now we are forty

'In Wilson's careful hands, via her deft and unobtrusive narrative, the stories of women in their forties, who have in common only a shared secondary school and age, come to life. What they reveal tells us much about how sex and socio-economic class shape life for women in Britain in the 2020s, making this book a significant social document for our times.'

– LISA DOWNING, author of *Selfish Women*

'Susannah Wilson has taken the temperature of her generation by producing this in-depth and fascinating insight into the lives of a group of midlife women. They reveal here their choices and chances, their experiences, their views, and the issues that concern them.'

– MARY INGHAM, author of *Now We Are Thirty*

'Wilson weaves from the stuff of her female subjects' everyday lives – their joys and sorrows, confusions, interconnections, and longings – a rich and compelling tapestry of women's lived experience in modern Britain. Her narrative illustrates in microcosm the shifting social and cultural forcefields that have pervaded women's lives ever since the sexual revolution, whilst raising tantalizing questions about what their daughters might still become.'

– MIRANDA GILL, author of *Eccentricity and the
Cultural Imagination in Nineteenth-Century Paris*

now we are forty

CONVERSATIONS WITH WOMEN

SUSANNAH WILSON

First published in paperback and eBook, 2023
by Seraphine Press

ISBN: 978-1-7394190-1-1 (paperback)
ISBN: 978-1-7394190-0-4 (eBook)

Editing, typeseting and cover design: Laura Kincaid,
Ten Thousand | Editing + Book Design
www.tenthousand.co.uk

A CIP catalogue record for this book is available
on request from the British Library

Printed and bound by Amazon

For Mary Ingham

Contents

Preface

Towards the end of 2015, when I was thirty-nine, I started thinking about what facing middle age meant for my generation of women. I set out to track down and interview the women who had been in my class at a suburban English comprehensive school in the 1990s, hoping to talk to them about life, family, work, love, and friendship as women approaching forty, at the cusp of the 2020s.

What had been the common experiences of our generation, growing up in the 1970s and '80s, becoming adults in the 1990s, and entering middle age in the late 2010s? I wanted to reflect on the education we had received, and on how our lives as women at the turn of the twenty-first century had differed from those of our mothers, who had grown up in the shadow of the Second World War, with fewer of the opportunities and freedoms we had enjoyed.

We sat our GCSE exams in 1992, when we were fifteen or sixteen, after which we parted company from the ones who left school while the rest of us stayed on to study A levels. How had our lives turned out? What are the lives of ordinary women like today? For those of us with daughters, how did we think their lives would be different from our own?

I happened to mention my idea for this project to a friend in the History Department at the university where I work. My colleague told me that a journalist called Mary Ingham had pursued the same thought in the 1970s, and in 1981 had published her first book, an oral history of British women – *Now We Are Thirty: Women of the Breakthrough Generation*.[1] Mary was born in 1947, at the height of the post-war baby 'bulge' generation, and five years after the birth of my own mother. *Now We Are Thirty* is a reflection on her childhood and youth, and on the experiences of other women from her class at grammar school. It deals with their childhood influences, ambitions, the work they would go on to do, the sexual revolution, motherhood, family, friendship, gender roles, and the state of relations between the sexes in 1970s Britain.

When I read *Now We Are Thirty* for the first time, it struck me that the big life questions that thirty-year-old women faced then map almost exactly onto those of fortysomething women today. As Mary wrote:

> Thirty, for a woman, is a sensitive age. [...] A childless thirty-year-old faces the fact that if she wants to start a family she hasn't got much time left, and perhaps, just as all these thoughts occur, her career is beginning to take off. A thirty-year-old mother finds her family beginning to grow out of their dependence on her and as they emphasize their individuality so she is forced to ponder her own. Who is she? What has she done with her life?[2]

Today, some forty years on, women tend to grapple with these same issues about a decade later in life. More women now start families in their thirties, with many delaying having children until after the age of thirty-five. By 2020, the majority of women turning thirty in the UK were childless – or 'child-free' as some prefer to call it, if it's an active choice.[3] Advances in fertility technologies have helped make it possible for women to have children later in life. But there is also, perhaps, a malaise in the younger generation today: for various socio-economic reasons, they seem to find it harder than ever to achieve autonomy, to find partners and make homes of their own, to start a family.

I wanted to write a book that in some way responded to Mary's, looking at the daughters born to her generation of women – that is, my generation, the girls born in the 1970s. As all projects do, this one grew legs, and what I have written has turned out to be a quite different book to the one Mary published. As she observed in *Now We Are Thirty*, children and books have in common 'the fact that each has a life of its own, you cannot control it, make it fit into what you thought it would be'.[4] Her book was in every way a personal and social historical reflection on her era, and on English women's lives in general. The main interest for me has turned out to be the individual life stories of the women I interviewed, and how they have negotiated the difficulties and the successes of their lives in the context of the social changes that have occurred since we were born. Now well into our forties, we are beginning to see our children grow up, and some have even left home. We face new challenges as we negotiate middle age.

I contacted Mary after reading her book, and we have corresponded and discussed my ideas over several years. I eventually met her in January 2016, and we talked at length about her original project. She shared with me some of her materials, such as the original questionnaires she had used. She also spoke frankly about some of the challenges of writing a book on such a personal topic. *Now We Are Thirty* continues to be an important part of Mary's legacy, her 'baby', as she calls it. She followed this book with one about the men of her generation, *Men* (Century, 1984). But her third book, *Facing Forty*, remains unfinished business. It focused again on the women of *Now We Are Thirty* a decade later, who, by the late 1980s, were reckoning with mid-life challenges. The book was commissioned. It was to be a discussion of issues then affecting forty-year-old women: the experience of ageing and loss of physical allure; infertility and childlessness; caring responsibilities and work issues; concluding with the challenges that lay ahead.

However, by this time, in addition to a prevailing belief that assumed women could 'have it all', the publishing industry was becoming more commercialized: so much so that *Facing Forty's* commissioning editor, seeing this change in her own publishing company, walked out. Although much of the *Facing Forty* research was done, and Mary had drafted some chapters, her new (and considerably younger) editor asked her to significantly alter the book, to produce a more superficial, self-help guide.

Instead, Mary abandoned *Facing Forty* and turned her attention elsewhere.

Mary shared with me one of the chapters she had drafted for *Facing Forty*. 'The Empty Nest' dealt unflinchingly with the experiences of certain women of her generation who lived the sexual liberation of the 1960s and '70s counterculture first-hand, delaying marriage and children. Naming them 'the walking wounded of feminism's second front', of which she was one, she wrote: 'We had rejected our parents' blueprint for life' and that, 'The aimless freedom we bought was expensive…' Reading what she wrote then, Mary says she would now qualify it: 'That freedom wasn't entirely aimless: we were in search of ourselves, as well as a meaningful, committed relationship. (In that sense, the men of our generation bear some responsibility, probably partly why my second book was about them.)'

Mary has mentored me in the writing of this book from beginning to end and has offered gentle encouragement throughout. Even though we have only once met face to face, she has nurtured this project, and it is, in some respects (although I'm not sure she would see it that way), the child of *Now We Are Thirty*. It has been a huge challenge to complete this book alongside full-time work and caring for young children, and all the usual crises that midlife hurls at women. It would not have been finished without Mary's generous engagement with my ideas, and her continual, quiet encouragement of the project. She has reminded me at times that abandoned projects can be painful, and that it is worth pushing through to the end. I have found that she is right.

Introduction

When Anne and I go out a walk,
We hold each other's hand and talk
Of all the things we mean to do
When Anne and I are forty-two

                 – A.A. Milne, *Now We Are Six*

There were about a hundred girls in our year at school. I will call it Highfield (not its real name). It was an ordinary comprehensive school, built in the early 1950s as a secondary modern, located at the border of the suburbs of London and the Home Counties. The building was red-brick, square, and boxy like many secondary schools of the era, and the grounds unprepossessing. It is located at the outer fringe of the 'gin and Jag' commuter belt that grew up around the capital in the decades after the Second World War, in the vicinity of mainline train stations. The new M25 motorway, which had opened two years before we arrived, passed through some local land that buttressed our school playing fields, and where we ran cross country – that typical peripheral London feature of motorways and dual carriageways running through nature reserves.[5]

Between 2017 and 2020, I recorded and transcribed interviews with ten women who had been in my year at school, nine of whom agreed that their stories could be included in this book. I have used pseudonyms instead of real names and have concealed place names to help protect the respondents' anonymity. Of those who do appear here, all were in some kind of paid work or career at the time of the interviews. Five were married, three were single, and one was in a long-term relationship. Seven had birth children, one had adopted two children, and one had chosen to be child-free. Five still lived in the area where we grew up, and four have moved away. Staying seems to be a more instinctive decision than leaving; many women want to live near friends and loved ones, and familiarity breeds attachment – even to unremarkable suburbs and cities. As Gareth E. Rees, chronicler of 'unofficial Britain' and its neglected landscapes, writes, 'Anybody should be able to feel a connection with place, no matter where they grew up or where they live, even in the densest concrete jungles or the most monotonous suburban sprawls.'[6]

Those who have moved away have done so with the active intention of wanting to re-establish their lives in a different place, all for different reasons. Five of us went to university after passing A levels, and four left school at sixteen. Of those who left school early, two went on to further education later in life, and two have never been to university. Kate was the first to have a baby, at nineteen, in 1995. Kim was the last to have a child, at forty-one, in 2017. Our children have been born across a span of more than twenty years but just about fit into the same generation. Women may have a certain commonality of experience, but their *feelings* about things like childbirth, caring for newborns, the baby stage, and their own personal journeys are unique – as their stories make clear.

In the late 1970s, Mary Ingham found that women who stayed at home to care for children were quite self-effacing and did not think that their lives were interesting:

> Housewives tend to underplay their world. So many women dismissed themselves with this label, protested that their lives were very boring within the first five minutes of our interview, that they lived from day to day and didn't do very much, and yet the thoughts and feelings winkled out of them show how much satisfaction they derive from their lives and how misleading the title of housewife really is.[7]

Almost forty years later, I found this was still a common belief, even among women who work outside the home. Most of the people I interviewed were faintly surprised that I was at all interested in their lives. 'Is that the kind of thing you want?' and 'My life is quite ordinary – I'm not sure it's that interesting' or 'My life is hardly exciting' were common reflections at the end of the interviews. But this book shows that everybody's life is interesting in some way and certainly unique.

In our conversations, we talked about the benefits of growing up in the 1990s – an era of theoretically equal opportunities – but also about the drawbacks for women of pursuing careers, and some of the unwanted consequences of being the first generation of women to break through in large numbers into what had previously been male-dominated workplaces. The situation with women's employment in the UK changed dramatically in the twenty-five years up until 2008, the year my first child was born, when I was thirty-one.[8] We had grown up in an era of comprehensive schooling, with low to middling academic expectations up to the age of sixteen. Kenneth Baker's Education Reform Act was passed in 1988, introducing a new National Curriculum, which our teachers were only beginning to get to grips with when we completed compulsory schooling.[9]

If we made it to sixth form to study A levels, the teaching was more focused and we were encouraged to apply to university, at a time (before the introduction of the first tuition fee in 1998) when higher education was still funded by the government via direct funding and student grants. When we went to university, we were treated as adults, and it had been a long time since the institution had acted 'in loco parentis', as it had in earlier generations. We enjoyed a period of unprecedented freedom when the stakes were low and the benefits high.

We grew up without social media, so our collective pressures were limited to time spent with friends, or at school, or perhaps in front of the television. I was twenty-two and beginning my final year at university in 1998 when I used email and the internet for the first time. I did not own a smartphone until after the birth of my first child, in 2008. As teenagers, lounging around aimlessly in our bedrooms was a common refuge, as was chatting to friends on the house phone. Our grandparents had all lived through the Second World War – an event that profoundly marked our parents' generation and, indirectly, our own. This affected us most through our parents' generally buttoned-up attitude to bringing us up – an observation that carries across the social classes.

Our mothers' generation was the last one in which it was the norm and even the expectation for women to give up their jobs when they had their first child, to stay home and care for husbands and children. They also felt more responsible than previous generations had for their children's psychological and emotional well-being.[10] Curiously, despite having been young in the liberal 1960s, our parents and teachers found it difficult to speak frankly to us about growing up – about puberty, sex, and sexuality. This was something that had not changed much in a generation, as Mary Ingham noted in the 1970s: 'Our mothers never discussed the practical problems of "snogging" with boys. They just loaded the responsibility on to us, as it had been dropped on to them.'[11]

Our parents' advice to us in the 1990s had been similarly vague and consisted in opaque warnings about not giving precious commodities away too easily (for girls) and being wary of a girl who made herself too available (for boys). Sexuality was not discussed in schools, although people were increasingly open about homosexuality from the late 1980s, and sex education was acknowledged by successive governments to be lacking in the curriculum.[12] The silence on sexuality in particular was due to Section 28 of the Local Government Act (1988) prohibiting the 'promotion of homosexuality' in schools under the Conservative government of Margaret Thatcher, the influence of which endured well beyond its repeal in England in 2003.[13]

The lives of the women whose stories are documented here coincided arbitrarily at a particular point in time: we had different social and class backgrounds and have gone on to have different life experiences. As case studies they are not representative of the full range of experiences of women of our generation, in terms of class, relative or absolute wealth, geography, or race.

But they are representative of a specific time and place, and their words form part of a human time capsule. The stories they tell suggest we lived through a period of opportunity and social mobility. But have we all equally? Myths around large-scale social mobility in Britain have been challenged by historians, but individual stories show that education has been crucial to securing a better future for women and their children.[14]

The women I spoke to, despite their trials and difficulties, have relatively successful lives by conventional standards. Some of the other women I contacted, who initially agreed to talk to me, pulled out – often at the last minute. They perhaps had less reason to want to pore over the details of their lives, which appear to have been more difficult. Some of them are now grandmothers, and others have experienced the breakdown of multiple relationships. Some regret having left school without qualifications. Others were in debt, or debilitated by chronic health problems, financial difficulties, a lack of familial support, alcohol and drug use, estrangement from their own children, or the reality of social services being involved in their lives. These are all common-enough situations faced by women today, but talking about these things – and putting their stories on the record – is a different matter. I wanted to mention them here though, because they are there, and their stories exist, even if I have been unable to tell them here. Some of them spoke briefly to me on the phone after expressing an interest in the project, and others answered some initial questions, but none ultimately felt able to sit down and have a recorded conversation.

The women who don't appear here have, of course, had their own struggles and triumphs. Many of their children have flourished, even where others have foundered. They often have that knack women seem to have of making something out of nothing, and of somehow surviving, and keeping on going. Several girls in our year at school had babies at fifteen or sixteen, but a number of them are now wary of discussing their lives, even though many of them did an excellent job of raising their children, and have managed to forge meaningful and secure lives, and to progress in the workplace. This is perhaps because, as contemporary historians have shown, unmarried mothers were uniquely politically vilified in the 1990s, and women who lived through that time fear the same judgement now.[15]

Labour MP Angela Rayner (Deputy Leader of the Opposition at the time of writing), who was born in 1980 and had a baby at sixteen, has spoken out about being publicly humiliated as a teenage mother.[16] Some of the women I write about in this book, who had babies very young, have also spoken about their fear of having their children taken from them, of not being trusted to care for them properly. One of the teen mums from our school told me she was banned by the deputy headmistress from bringing her baby into school to 'show everyone', lest it give the rest of us ideas. Shame is a powerful social mechanism. She was a bad example, and she knew it. These girls were supposed to be ashamed, not proud. But isn't it common for mothers to feel proud of their babies, when they love them so much, and to want others to share in their happiness?

Despite this enduring shame, what *had* changed between our mothers' generation and ours was society's view on sex outside of marriage and single motherhood more generally. Although unmarried mothers remained stigmatized (even when they were not even single, as Kate's story will show), in our generation it became the norm for women to have more than one sexual partner before settling down to have a family, and for couples to live together before marriage, although this remained a controversial issue for traditional families. There are now almost exactly the same number of children born outside of wedlock as within,[17] which contrasts with our mothers' youth when sexual experience before marriage had generally been 'a guilty secret, a private tryst between engaged couples'.[18] By the 1990s, it was highly unusual for couples to wait for marriage for sex, although the sexual double standard remained; it would still give a girl a 'reputation' to sleep around, but the social standing of boys was not similarly sullied by casual sex. It was easy for us, as a generation of young women, to access contraception (the pill had originally only been available to married women) and abortion, if necessary, so we had a measure of control over these elements of our lives.

The women featured in this book were all born between 1 September 1975 and 31 August 1976; I was one of the youngest, born at the very end of this period. We started school – infants, as we called it – in 1980–81, as 'rising fives'. The area where we lived still had the middle school system, so we went up to secondary school at the age of twelve, rather than eleven, which for us was the school year 1988–89. Because there were a lot of prestigious private schools in the area where we lived, on the outskirts of London, the local comprehensives often had terrible reputations. Ours was considered 'fine', the sort of place where bright children could do well, even if it was a little rough around the edges.

There were, just outside our area, some grammar schools that you could apply to, but most people didn't. There were also former grammar schools (that became comprehensives) that rode on their former reputations and were thought to be the better schools. And there were a few Girls' Day School Trust schools that had offered direct-grant grammar provision, but which were by the 1980s all private (although they still offered assisted places and scholarships).[19] It was all very complicated and most parents, like mine, just sent their children to one of the local comprehensives without getting too concerned with the vagaries of a highly idiosyncratic system.

Most of the former classmates I interviewed agree the education we received was adequate; there were opportunities offered, but we did not all have the maturity, judgement, or support to make good decisions. To succeed academically at most comprehensive schools, you needed one of two things: either a high level of parental investment in your education or exceptional self-motivation. To do very well, you usually needed both – and a sprinkling of luck.

I have sometimes felt quite negative about comprehensive schooling, but I now realize it did offer a good start for most pupils. By conventional metrics at least, we can claim good outcomes from the mixed education we received: many of us have enjoyed professional successes, achieved financial security, attended excellent universities, and gained the highest of academic qualifications. Leaving school with a set of GCSEs is often the key to social mobility later in life, as the accounts related in this book show.[20] It is of course possible to achieve career success without basic educational qualifications, but it is harder, rarer, and it takes longer. This said, these women's stories also make the case that other accomplishments – personal and interpersonal, spiritual, and creative – are equally significant markers of a life well lived.

We were the fourth cohort of pupils to take GCSEs, which had replaced O levels and CSEs in England in 1988, and in 1992, the year we sat our exams, the government first published schools' exam results. Our school, I vaguely recall, had solid, but not brilliant, stats – about 50 per cent of children passed five GCSEs at grades A–C. I managed to track down an archive of Highfield school newsletters, but these did not start until 1994, the year I took my A levels. The September 1994 issue states that the school's GCSE results were 'well above the national average', without giving an exact figure. Reading between the lines, I think the omission suggests that our results were lower than some of the other local secondary schools. But the school was proud to be a 'true comprehensive', where all pupils were entered for the exams, even if they were not expected to get top grades. The national average in 1992 was 38.3 per cent at grades A–C.[21] Visibly, for half the children at our school, and for 61.7 per cent of children nationally, five pass grades at GCSE was out of reach. These data seem to be an indictment of an educational system from which most children emerged as exam failures, on paper at least – one in which those who succeeded also felt like a besieged minority.

Those of us who stayed on to do A levels took them in 1994. Some of us went on to university in 1994–95, and so started on career paths in the late 1990s, towards the year 2000. We were still young then, but as I finish writing this, in 2022, we are, at forty-five, middle-aged. We are technically considered part of Generation X, although we only caught the tail end of it, and we overlap culturally with Millennials.[22] The great difference between the two generations is that Gen X grew up entirely without the internet and mobile phones – these arrived in the late 1990s, by which time we'd reached adulthood. Our parents are, almost without exception, part of the 'baby boomer' or the 'bulge' generation, born between 1946 and 1952, although some older parents would have been born during the Second World War.[23] My mother was born in 1942, and I was her third child – so she was nearly thirty-four when I was born, in 1976. But most people in the 1970s had children in their twenties, the average age for a woman to have her first baby in 1975 being twenty-four.

Our school was located in the middle of a council estate in which a proportion of the houses would have been sold off under Thatcher's 'Right to Buy' scheme, introduced by the 1980 Housing Act. By the end of 1987, the year we were finishing primary school, 1.1 million former council tenants had become homeowners, and the number of properties inhabited by owner-occupiers was on the rise – from 55 per cent in 1979 to 70 per cent in 2003.[24] In our neighbourhood, part of the Tory heartlands, the policy was rather popular, and people seemed proud to become homeowners, but the social housing stock was often not replenished in line with need and demand. Ours is still a generation of owner-occupiers overall, but things are changing, and many younger people today think they will never own a home.[25]

There was, I recall, a chip shop and a Chinese takeaway at the end of the road where our school was located. There was also a 'rec' – a recreation ground – a large, flat square of grass with a football pitch and a faintly dilapidated kids' playground in the corner. There was a metal railway footbridge behind the rec, and on the opposite corner to the park, there was a typical suburban, interwar pub called something like The Royal Standard, which I heard has now closed.

The recent crisis and decline of the suburban British pub would have seemed unimaginable for people of our generation. The pub has been in a slow decline since the 1930s, but it was still the social fulcrum of many people's lives in post-war Britain, right up to the end of the 2000s, across classes and other political and social groups, although of course women were only really welcome in them from the mid-1980s.[26] Every tribe had its pub, and every school had its unofficial 'local' by the time we were in sixth form. There were rockers' pubs, 'crusty' pubs, pubs for the 'posh' private-school kids, estate pubs, gay pubs, country pubs, and, most importantly for us fifth- and sixth-formers, those with a reputation for serving underage teenagers. Perhaps the widely documented drinking problem among members of Generation X owes something to this embedded pub culture. The children of iGen and younger, who have grown up with the internet as their social playground, have never had the same need to social-ize in pubs and on average drink less than we did. For us, it was one of the main places to meet people.

Our parents came from a wide range of different occupations and social classes. They were postmen and women, cleaners, electricians, carpenters, gardeners, shop workers, doctors, sec-retaries, university professors, vicars, and stay-at-home mothers with 'little jobs'. A few were unemployed, but in an area of high employment, the less well off were more likely to be in one or several low-paid jobs. Our school lacked the children of the very wealthy and the upper-middle classes, although somebody once told me that the children of an '80s pop group had attended our school. But first, I don't know if that's true; and second, I'm not sure how wealthy being one member of a briefly popular '80s band would make you. The more obviously wealthy were the self-made rich – people who'd made money in the trades or in property. The children of the wealthier, educated upper-middle classes tended to be sent to one of the numerous prestigious private schools in the wider county.[27]

As I now realize, our school was less socially mixed than I thought at the time. According to the 2001 census, 92.1 per cent of British people described themselves as white. Although in London a higher percentage (20 per cent) of people were from an ethnic minority, our secondary school was in the outer sub-urbs and was not very ethnically diverse.[28] My primary school, which was several miles closer to London, was significantly more mixed than the secondary school, located on the city side of the M25. As second- and third-generation members of ethnic minorities move into the middle and upper-middle classes, these areas are gradually and organically diversifying.

Several of the women I interviewed grew up on another estate a few miles from our school. It had been built in the 1970s and they were the first families to live in the three-bedroom family homes it provided. All my interviewees who lived there talk about it in effusively positive tones and describe a system of social housing that worked well at the time, providing good-quality, low-rent accommodation for people on lower incomes and their families.[29] Although many of those I spoke to were not wealthy, and still are not, none was desperately poor, and we lived in an affluent part of the country. In contrast to many parts of the UK, in our town it was possible for most young people to find work upon leaving school.

We were insulated from the massive decline of heavy industry and the political malaise that so marked parts of the UK in the 1980s, although one of the enduring memories of my childhood is the daily headlining of the 1984–85 miners' strike on the BBC's six o'clock news, watched religiously by my parents and most of the family. The images etched in my mind are of the black colliery wheels rising into a bleak, overcast sky; crowds of young lads in jeans and donkey jackets facing off with police officers in smart, black uniforms; the beat-up buses carrying the men breaking the strike across picket lines to go to work; women ladling out food in church halls, working men's clubs and community centres for the hungry strikers and their families. Some of my friends had fathers who worked in the Metropolitan Police, and they were called upon to police the miners' strike. We weren't sure which side we were on, and it felt like it was all happening a long way away, which mostly it was.

The fact that we lived in a region largely unaffected by this industrial strife probably explains the enduring support for the Conservative government through the 1980s and '90s in the Home Counties. With high employment, it was a system that worked reasonably well for all but the most vulnerable, and it was easy for people to believe that their affluence was down to individual hard work rather than other factors, such as luck, or the opportunities provided by the immense economic dominance of the capital city in an era before the significant devolution of political power to the individual nations of the UK.[30]

Yet, the 1980s and '90s were also decades of great political conflict and desire for change, which would ultimately be delivered by Labour's landslide election victory under Tony Blair in 1997. This was the first election we were eligible to vote in, when we were twenty-one. I was in my second year at university in Manchester and we filled the student union bar into the night, feverishly awaiting the result we all seemed to want. (We did of course have friends who were Conservatives; they just tended to keep quiet when the other side was in the ascendant, and they certainly didn't come to the bar on election night.) In the 1992 election, John Major had only just – and unexpectedly – won a slim majority for the Conservatives, so for those of us who had grown up knowing the Thatcher government, the change felt long overdue.

In our generation, ordinary people who were happy to send their children to the local school generally believed that their progeny would grow up well enough without too much parental interference. It was common for children to walk to school alone or with siblings or friends from the age of about six, and to play out for hours at a stretch in the street or in playgrounds, or local countryside, with a gang of other local children. The freedom we had was normal for our generation, and a common feature of the lives of many kids across the world.[31]

Many of the women I write about in this book vividly remember this aspect of our lives. We were the last of the free-range generations, who roamed small neighbourhoods in groups, before the neurotic over-protectionism of 1990s and 2000s parenting.[32] We took the bus on our own, cycled long distances unaccompanied, and went on the train to London to go shopping or sightseeing with friends or siblings well before the age of sixteen. Our parents seemed to think we were old enough to manage these things by ourselves.

I would also argue that, due perhaps to our parents' laissez-faire approach and our freedom from social media and the internet, our generation of women growing up was much less concerned with stereotypically feminine modes of self-presentation, gender roles, and inner identity and how to outwardly project that. As young children, especially for those of us whose mothers were feminists, we wore the same hand-me-downs and short haircuts, and many girls were comfortable being tomboys.[33] As we grew older, we girls (and some boys) liked to experiment with clothes, outlandish hairstyles, and make-up, but if you wanted to take a photo of yourself, you had to first finish the camera film, then take the film capsule to Boots to be developed, then pay £3.99 and wait a week before you could pick up the pictures, which were inevitably and unalterably terrible and which could not be 'liked'. This was not a motivating sequence of events. As a result, we were preoccupied with, but not obsessed by, our appearance to others, and it was certainly not interesting to anyone else.

A common view in my conversations was that our rather laid-back schooling, with some notable exceptions, left us with a vague lack of confidence in our abilities. Several of the women I talked to mentioned 'imposter syndrome' – that they feel like frauds who don't deserve the success they've achieved. This is a particular problem for women in higher education, about which entire books have been written.[34]

Girls and women seem to be particularly sensitive to criticism and early experiences of failure, and when we push through the natural inclination to shrink away, we often feel like imposters. Words of encouragement at school were rare, although we do owe the school some credit here, because if many of us were able to aspire to more than our parents had done or achieved, it must be in part because the school created an environment in which children could be gently shown to aim higher. It might not have been Eton, but it wasn't a sink or a swamp either. Many of our teachers cared deeply about our progress and had ambitions for us, but I'm not sure we noticed this clearly at the time. Despite the desire to raise our expectations, our teachers were operating in a school context in which, as the stories told in this book reveal, people were intensely aware of their place in the overall class hierarchy.

Our generation was the last one to benefit from free further and higher education for several years after we left school. This allowed women, especially those who had children very young, to access education later in life without having to incur debts upwards of £50,000, as do today's students. These opportunities were precious, and they do not exist today in the same way, and some of those stories are told here.

Tuition fees of £1,000 were introduced in September 1998 under the Blair Labour government and increased to £3,000 in 2004. These eventually, of course, were increased further to £9,000 in September 2012.[35] The astronomical cost of higher education has changed entirely the landscape of university study. Some of the women I interviewed for this book said that they would not have attended university if the cost had been as high as it is today. The era in which we were young was a time of opportunity for people who lacked parental support when it came to accessing higher education. The stories told in this book, especially by Emily and Emma, testify to the value of this opportunity.

In these conversations we talk about family, friendship, growing up, relationships, the education of women and girls, and work and careers. All the women I spoke to, whether or not they have biological children of their own, said that they gained great fulfilment from caring for and being involved in the raising of children. But one recurring pinch point for so many women is the difficulty of combining work with caring for children. This is particularly acute for single mothers. Some of them seem to have solved this by taking a step back from their former careers, although it's clear they also derived a huge amount of satisfaction from the work they did before having children. Others, like me, work full-time in demanding careers and are left feeling that they are only able to function at 75 per cent in each role, leaving them feeling stretched beyond normal capacity, to 150 per cent overall. And as our children grow older, we realize that they still need us just as much.

If we're to achieve the necessary balance between work and family life, it is clear that we need further major structural change in the workplace. Rebecca Asher argues that we need 'to discover if there is another way of organizing our homes, communities and workplaces which would enable both women and men to give wholeheartedly to their children and to experience the joy of a deep connection with them, while retaining other fulfilling elements of their lives'.[36] Similarly, Megan K. Stack highlights how many women are 'saddled with disproportionate work at home' and 'too embarrassed to say it out loud'. They often then feel inadequate for *not* managing to do it all: 'It's proof that we are not sufficiently devoted to our children or to our careers, depending on who's doing the judging. It is proof – and there is ever more proof – that we ourselves are not sufficient.'[37]

This book considers what has changed for women since our mother's generation turned forty, in the 1980s, and what has stayed the same. Our mothers grew up and became young adults before the legal advances brought about by the Sex Discrimination and Equal Pay Acts, and the establishment of the Equal Opportunities Commission. The Employment Protection Act of 1975 guaranteed paid maternity leave under certain conditions, and the right to return to work within 29 weeks of childbirth. As our mothers generally left the workforce during the years when they had a young family, only a minority of them would have benefitted from these changes. Nevertheless, they did live through an era of great change in which these things were made possible.[38]

Despite addressing some very difficult themes, most of these conversations ended on an upbeat note. Although it is certainly not the case for *all* women of our age, for those I did speak to, at least, it seems that forty is a good life stage and we feel better than we ever have, despite our ageing bodies. As Mary Ingham observed in *Facing Forty*: 'mature women have acquired something in exchange for crow's feet and "expression lines". We have a certain toughness, a certain strength and self-confidence, a certain fire inside us; we are not so easily going to put up with the constraints so many mature women before us had to suffer.'[39]

The 'breakthrough generation' certainly blazed a trail for us. Before examining more closely the lives of my schoolfriends, a group of women who met when they were twelve and who are now in their forties, I begin by turning to look at my own life and history, and to the lives of my mother and grandmothers, in order to better understand the roots of my generation of women.

1

My Grandmother, My Mother, Myself

My maternal grandmother, Ivy Florence, was born in London in 1913 and died when she was ninety-three, in 2006. Her birth certificate states that she was born in Camberwell, and it records her father's occupation as 'labourer'. Ivy was the youngest of four children, two girls and two boys, and the family lived on the Old Kent Road in South East London. She was from the same generation as Mary Ingham's mother, born in 1907 – another member of 'the mute, martyred generation of our mums, blanked out in the diary of women's history'.[40]

One of the last times I saw my grandmother, I spoke to her at some length about her life. She still had a strong London accent even in old age, although she'd lived in Kent for most of her adult life. Ivy wanted to be a nurse, but her family couldn't afford for her to stay in school to complete her training. In this era, working-class girls were expected to complete only elementary education. Before the passing of the 1944 Education Act, which set the blueprint for education in post-war Britain and opened up education to girls and the lower classes, children like Ivy usually left school at fourteen.[41]

Mary Ingham noted that homemaking skills had been the pinnacle of her own mother's education: 'In their final year, when they were fourteen, they had two full days of domestic training per week, one in the kitchen and one in the laundry.'[42] Girls' secondary education was established in the late nineteenth century, but 'it was considered an unnecessary luxury for most girls who would, after all, only become housewives'.[43]

Ivy also lived in an era in which girls, in addition to doing paid work or attending school, were expected to work harder than boys in the home, as observed in a report published in 1926 by the Board of Education.[44]

Like so many of her contemporaries, my grandmother left school at fourteen (which she always said was because her older sister, Violet, had fallen pregnant and had a child out of wedlock, leaving the family to support them both) and went to work in the laundry at a fever hospital. She lived in Peckham, so I believe this must have been the Park Fever Hospital at Hither Green, a short bus ride from her home, or a thirty-minute walk.[45] This would have been in 1927–28, when she was still a child. It was the era before the establishment of the NHS and the advent of the antibiotics and vaccines we now take for granted.

The job of the laundry women was to wash the bedsheets of children who were gravely ill with the main infectious diseases of the era: diphtheria, scarlet fever, whooping cough, measles, and tuberculosis. The sick children were brought to the hospital in yellow 'fever vans' to be isolated for several weeks until no longer infectious, or until they died.[46] My grandmother said she remembered children being carried in from the vans four to a stretcher; others were abandoned outside the hospital to be brought in by nurses and porters.

Ivy's childhood in the interwar period, and mine in the 1980s, could not have been more different. Although I grew up in a draughty vicarage and we didn't have a lot of material possessions, we had central heating and hot running water, plenty of food, clothes, and space. Children in families like my grandmother's had one set of clothes, one pair of shoes, a bath once a week, and food was sometimes scarce. I do not think Ivy would ever have considered herself a feminist; I imagine she considered the women's movement a fringe concern of upper-middle-class women. She accepted traditional gender roles, but she was always bitter about having to leave school so young and missing out on the opportunity to become a nurse; the same seeds of the radical discontent expressed by 'second-wave' feminists (who focused on political and social equality) were in her too.

She met my grandfather, Denis, when they were in their early twenties and they worked and saved up money for several years before they married, to afford rent for a small house. This was typical of the times in which they lived: couples in the 1920s and '30s married later than their children would in the 1950s and '60s.[47] After her marriage, Ivy gave up working and became a housewife. Denis had also grown up in nearby Lewisham and attended the local boys' grammar school.

My grandparents were aspirational working-class Londoners who moved to Tonbridge in Kent, and into the lower-middle classes, just before the war. They hoped for a son but had two daughters – my mother in 1942 and her younger sister in 1944. The family lived in a small, newly built council house when their children were young; only much later in life could they afford to buy a modest newbuild house in a village near Tunbridge Wells.

Denis worked in middle management as a buyer for a tile manufacturer and enjoyed the post-war job security this provided. He used to say, a little ironically, 'Live in Kent and be content,' or, 'Live in Surrey free from worry,' citing the post-war Southern Railway advertising features that encouraged people to move out of London to the expanding suburbs. This was the journey many of our families had made.

My maternal grandparents were frugal people who lived simple, quiet lives. They both enjoyed handcrafts. Denis was an accomplished wood worker who also loved working on his allotment; Ivy enjoyed knitting, sewing, and baking. When they were young adults, they converted to the Plymouth Brethren, a rather austere, non-conformist, non-denominational Protestant church. My grandfather was a pacifist and conscientious objector during the Second World War. He was required to join the war effort on the home front, which meant being sent away for long periods to work on farms, leaving Ivy alone at home to care for their young daughters.

Faith was central to their lives; they lived, in a quiet way, separately from what they considered a corrupt world. They were always teetotal – a reaction against the waste and destruction wrought by alcoholism among the working classes they had grown up within. They were honest people who did their best with what they had, and aspired for more for their children and grandchildren.

There was a gulf of experience between their generation, who sacrificed so much during the Second World War (whether or not they physically fought in combat), and my mother's generation, who enjoyed peace and prosperity, despite the emotional deprivation associated with growing up in the post-war era.

My paternal grandmother, Margaret, was born in Birmingham in 1919 into a family of gold- and silversmiths. At nineteen she fell in love with the local young Anglican curate, my grandfather William Wilson. They married in July 1939, on her twentieth birthday. Margaret went on to have four children in five years, between 1942 and 1948. She finished school and worked for a few years before she married, during the interwar period when life was very difficult for most families.

Margaret had to hand over every penny she earned as a secretary to her parents. The responsibility placed on women to support their families financially once of working age was an experience my grandmothers shared, but they were also expected to give up work when they married. During the depression years of the 1930s, this was an actual legal bar.[48] When she married, Margaret took on the role of vicar's wife, which was a vocation in itself. It was generally frowned upon for clergy wives to take paid work.[49]

William and Margaret spent most of their married life in St John's Wood in London, where my grandfather was a dynamic and well-regarded vicar. They moved to the Scottish Highlands when their first grandchild was born, and we saw them very rarely after that – every two or three years, I recall.

My grandfather, as an Anglican parish priest, was not called up to serve in the Second World War, but he too was occupied working towards the war effort at home, on night watches and busy with parish work. Money was tight, and I am told that the family were in debt and at risk of bankruptcy for several years. Much of William's clergy stipend was spent on parish entertaining and helping parishioners in desperate need. They consequently struggled at times to adequately clothe and feed their own children, and to heat their enormous, glacially cold vicarage. They lived in genteel poverty.

Some of their financial woes were the result of their upper-middle-class expectations: their four children were all privately educated, because sending them to city schools alongside working-class children was considered inappropriate, although my father and some of his siblings managed to get music scholarships, and other people – friends, wealthy parishioners, and relatives – helped out with the fees.

The children also had private music lessons, and the family employed a daily 'help' to keep up with cleaning and housework. With four young children, Margaret employed au pairs from Europe to help her. This was perhaps an economical option for a family who had a large house but little spare money. My uncle, Clive Wilson, who left the UK in the 1960s for the US to pursue a career as a jazz musician in New Orleans, says in his own published memoir that my grandfather was a product of the Edwardian era. He believed that parents should avoid affection and displays of emotion: 'My mother later told me that when she was a young mother, she was quite influenced by this advice from both my father and her in-laws and was often torn between that and following her own instincts.'[50]

Elizabeth, my aunt, recalls vicarage life as especially tough for the girls: 'Margaret called me her "right hand", which meant continual housework at weekends, Sunday School, help with catering for parish lunches and teas then washing up with my sister afterwards; cleaning brass and silver, darning socks, food shopping, cooking.' Married women could not easily prevent pregnancies, and my grandmother struggled to cope with the children she already had. Margaret opted to have her 'tubes tied' when still in her twenties. She was therefore among the first generation of women to access sterilization for contraception, which was used clinically (rather than experimentally) for the first time in 1930.[51]

Margaret apparently suffered mentally, especially when she went through the menopause. Resources were scarce across society, and little could be done to help women in distress. They were simply not a priority.

My father, who was sent away to boarding school at the age of seven, had a distant relationship with his parents. The siblings have always been closer, and despite their relative privilege, they were all left feeling deprived by their childhood experiences.

When my mother, Mavis, was born in 1942, her parents were very disappointed to have a girl. Despite this setback, they were always ambitious for their daughters and proud they both passed the eleven plus for admission to Tonbridge Grammar School for Girls.

My mother has told me that going to grammar school was liberating, as it offered an alternative to the restricted world view of her parents. Although my mother's Christian faith has always been a feature of her life, in young adulthood she rejected the tradition of the Brethren, who believed every word of the Bible to be literally true.

We used to live near a Brethren congregation in the city where I now live, and, on sunny Sundays, its members would gather outside the church building. It was striking to see many women in their teens and early twenties married with children already, distinguishable by their uniform of long, full skirts and little blue headscarves. It is easy, as a feminist, to sneer at this way of life and to shudder at the idea of being a mere 'handmaiden', a baby machine whose purpose it is to continue to populate a traditional, closed community. It is harder to understand what women gain from living in communities with these rigidly prescribed gender roles and what they stand to lose in rejecting them. Despite the reality of patriarchal hierarchies, women in traditional communities are supported by their menfolk and each other, and they are rarely alone. But neither are they allowed or encouraged to work outside the home or to choose alternative lifestyles to marriage, homemaking, and motherhood.

My grandparents expected their daughters to be well educated, and their hope was for them to marry well, find young men with excellent, professional job prospects who were in good standing in the church. I don't think they intended their daughters to pursue careers, but this was the path their mid-twentieth-century education put them on.

Life at home was quite restricted for my mother. Church on Sunday, and no playing games or activity other than rest, reading, and contemplation. The girls went to school, did their homework, played the piano, and read books. There was not a lot of socializing with other children and their lives were quite solitary. My mother certainly didn't enjoy many of the freedoms other girls were starting to enjoy in the 1950s and '60s, which Mary Ingham talked about in *Now We Are Thirty*: 'It was still unthinkable for a girl to go out on her own, like the boys could, but unlike our French and German pen-friends we had the freedom to go out in the evening to church hall dances, just a group of girls.'[52] My mother did not experience this level of freedom until she left home.

The girls at my mother's grammar school were strongly encouraged to go to university. Their teachers had been part of the first generation of female graduates at British universities, as Mary Ingham described them, a 'clique of single women teachers, long hair firmly controlled under a hairnet and twisted into plaits or a bun, long box-pleated tweedy skirts and sturdy lace-up shoes'.[53] Attending university was unusual in a time when most bright young women were encouraged into teaching, nursing and secretarial work.

My mother did go to university to study English, and she gained a first-class degree in an era before the Sex Discrimination Act was passed and it was legal for universities to prioritize men over women in admissions.[54] My mother trod a middle path between her traditional, conservative Christian upbringing and modern feminism. She welcomed initiatives such as equal pay and legal action against discrimination, but she was certainly not part of the 1960s counterculture and has lived a conventional life in terms of marriage and family.

My father was a young Anglican curate when they married and my mother's vocation also, for a time, became that of the vicar's wife. Their four children were born between 1971 and 1979. Later, once we had all started school, my mother started theological training herself, and was among the first cohort of women to be ordained as deaconesses in the late 1980s and as priests in 1994.[55] She has always been a strong feminist role model, and she finished her career in her sixties as rector of a thriving Anglican parish. She was in her element and seemed happiest when working full-time, in charge of a large congregation.

She has always worn her femininity lightly and tends to be more comfortable in everyday wear rather than dressing up for occasions. Though she is always well turned out, I have always found it quite liberating that my mother is not too interested in feminine preening. She has taught me that these elements of self-presentation do not matter much, and that the most important thing about a person is their mind, and the relationships they forge, the work they do, and how they treat other people.

I was born in our local district hospital on 13 August 1976, the third of four children, during one of the driest and hottest summers in modern British history. My mother tells me that the birth was quick and easy. There aren't many pictures of me as a baby, nor of my younger sister, born in 1979, but our home was a happy one, full of people and other children.

My mother is very sociable and loves to keep busy. While we were young, she set up and ran a local playgroup and was actively involved in community activities centred around the lives of women, such as the Mothers' Union and Young Wives. The names of these groups sound quaint these days, but they could be quite radical. They were often about educating women on the pressing issues of the day and advocating for women's rights. They facilitated social networking and were, for politically committed women, an intellectually stimulating place to meet likeminded people at a similar life stage.

I am told that the playgroup she set up and ran in the 1970s was affiliated to the Preschool Playgroups Association, now the Early Years Alliance.[56] There was very little in the way of state nursery provision, and these playgroups were grassroots organizations set up by women – typically mothers of young children themselves – who wanted to provide good quality childcare. They used to run in the mornings and were focused on the needs of young children, and did not provide full day-care. Playgroup gave women a couple of hours in the morning to run errands or attend appointments, to socialize without children present, or to get on with housework. They were designed to give children a high-quality, play-based learning experience, and the philosophy behind them aligned with the Montessori model of early-years education. They prepared children for school and gave them the opportunity to interact with other children and to learn through tactile play.

My parents and many of their contemporaries, in some contrast to their own parents' Edwardian sensibilities, generally embraced the ideas of 1960s childcare guru Dr Benjamin Spock and the psychoanalyst John Bowlby, whose ideas about the importance of love, play, physical touch, and secure attachment were popular.[57] Although my parents were conservative in terms of sexual morality, ideas from radical 1960s counterculture certainly trickled down to the parenting practices of their era.

I remember attending the playgroup, and I think it was a very happy time for me. I sometimes attribute my lifelong love of languages to meeting bilingual children there. I made a friend called Charlotte who was half French, and met a little boy whose mother was Dutch. I was fascinated by the fact that they could apparently speak two languages. These two children were extremely quiet though, and on reflection I wonder if they couldn't yet speak English, despite my best efforts at communicating loudly with them. It did become my life's ambition to be bilingual.

My father, who sadly died in 2013, was an Anglican vicar in charge of a large and vibrant congregation in a town a few miles away from my secondary school. We moved to the vicarage when I was five, in 1981, and my parents lived there until I was midway through my university course, in 1997. The only thing my dad really wanted for us, educationally, was *never* to be sent to boarding school like he had been. My parents' version of Christianity was small-c socially conservative, politically liberal, or left-wing, and tinged with feminism. I recall my older siblings joking that our mother might abandon us to join the anti-nuclear Peace Camps at Greenham Common, and I have sometimes wondered if she felt a genuine dilemma about this.

In another life, without children, perhaps my mother would have been more of an activist. Margaret Thatcher was Prime Minister for the entire decade in which we grew up, and was broadly popular where we lived, but my parents disliked what they perceived to be the selfish individualism of that Conservative government's policies. We believed in helping other people, and, as part of our family commitment to living in community, we often took people into our home to live, sometimes for long periods, when they needed it. The vicarage was an open house, and as such there was never a dull moment, but it wasn't always easy for us children to accommodate these other people and their life crises.

Growing up in the vicarage, we had an enormous garden and an outbuilding that had been the stables for the old house, with a huge ancient oak tree that came down in the great storm of 1987, when I was eleven. My younger sister and I played outside a lot, and we created endless imaginary games in the dusty stable hayloft. The vicarage was always full of people and animals, with several litters of kittens over the years, and it was used for parish business as well as church socializing.

My parents were quite countercultural in their values; they believed in living in community with others, and in sharing possessions and money, and in creating a wide extended family of people centred on the church. When it came out in 2000, I watched the Lukas Moodysson film *Together*, a comedy-drama about living in a hippy commune in 1970s Sweden, and the scene felt very familiar. We children all went to the local state primary school, which was very laid-back (you could, as I discovered, spend all your time in the reading corner avoiding doing maths).

Primary school was happy enough because there was little pressure and no strong expectations. As others in this book will testify, the early years were mostly about playing and learning how to socialize. Although we were taught to read and basic mathematics, there was an emphasis on storytelling, craft, art, singing, playing games outside and only mildly competitive sports.

My secondary school was a few miles away from where we lived. I cycled to school in all weathers; this is a discomfort I still put myself through to this day! The two nearest second-ary schools were single sex, both former grammar schools, and although they had good reputations academically, my parents wanted us to go to mixed secondary schools. They had both been educated in exclusive, single-sex environments and wanted something different for their own children. It's ironic in a way, because their egalitarian principles meant that they rejected the elite kind of education from which they had benefitted. But I wonder sometimes if I would have been happier at the girls' school. My primary-school friends went there, and although they avoided the harassment we got from boys, I expect the girl bullies would have been just as bad. But for some girls there are real benefits to single-sex education, as Mary Ingham reflected:

> I'm glad I went to a single sex school. We had our own world, and you could go right to the top of it. With the boys I feel sure we should have shrunk into the old stereotypes, where they forged ahead while we froze into giggling self-consciousness or frittered ourselves away on dog-like devoted attentiveness in class. They would have claimed physics and chemistry, leaving us to potter on with soft-bellied biology, and of course the arts.[58]

Going up to secondary school in 1988 was challenging for all of us, moving from a small, caring and personalized environment into a faceless mass of people, some of whom could be a little aggressive. I found the physical environment depressing; the school was run-down (it was the 1980s, after all…), dank, dark and a bit cold. I was embarrassed about my dad being a vicar. Luckily for me, our school was not on my dad's 'patch' for school assemblies, and so I was spared the indignity of having to listen to his sermons alongside my friends as a teenager.

Adolescence was tricky, as it often is. Like many girls, I felt awkward about puberty and didn't really talk to my mother about it. It wasn't that she was not willing to talk; I was just very reserved about it. I did have good friends – from school and church youth group – through my teenage years, which helped because we could laugh together about our plight. There was a lot of time to waste, since I didn't spend a lot of it doing homework or sport or music or other structured activities. As teenagers we had freedom to roam, and favourite activities included the thrills of 'late-night shopping' on Thursday evenings at the local shopping centre, and hours spent watching TV.

We'd also go clothes shopping (if we had money) at the local Saturday indoor market. At school I was considered able but inattentive and a bit lazy – my teachers' reports note that I was chatty, forgetful, and chronically late. Choice remarks include: 'Susie sometimes seems reluctant to put herself out', 'wastes time in idle chatter', 'not always achieving her best' and 'much more effort needed'. My favourites are the withering comments made by my French teacher: 'Susannah's French is good. It is a pity she does not always make the necessary effort to achieve better results.' The shame this induced in me meant that I eventually trained myself out of these bad habits.

Today, I think children who struggle with distraction and personal organization are better understood by schools. I did get there in the end, but it took a lot of effort on my part. I didn't discover the pleasures of reading in depth and at length until I was an older teenager.

Saturdays were taken up with things like swimming lessons and shopping trips where we aimlessly traipsed around towns, wasting the little bits of money we had, sometimes buying clothes and cassette tapes in record stores (sometimes vinyl), occasionally stealing make-up from Superdrug. Along with most older children in the UK, we recorded the weekly singles charts on Radio 1 every Sunday afternoon onto tapes and had posters of 1980s pop icons on our bedroom walls. We used to ride around the local rec on our bikes, and to and from each other's houses. When we were a bit older, maybe about fourteen, we'd go to Pizza Hut and buy the cheapest pizza on the menu and a Coke for £2.99.

Most of my girlfriends read all of Judy Blume's books before graduating to the deeply age-inappropriate Virginia Andrews' *Flowers in the Attic* series, featuring child imprisonment, sadistic violence, torture and incest. We started off on *Girl* magazine at eleven and moved onto *Just Seventeen* when we were about thirteen. These publications instructed us on suitable outfits for a first date (I don't recall anyone having 'a date' – it seemed to be the stuff of American teen magazine fantasy) and general make-up tips, and of course there was the advice of the agony aunt to help with problems like spots and falling out with friends. It seems like an age of innocence compared to the sado-masochistic sex tips handed out these days in *Teen Vogue*.

I think most people who attend large comprehensive schools feel like an anonymous number, rather than an individual, for the first few years at least. French was one of my better subjects, despite my teachers' despairing predictions, and by A level we were taught in small classes by enthusiastic women who were keen Francophiles. During the summer after my GCSEs, I did a month-long exchange with a French girl who lived in the suburbs of Paris. For both of us, it was a transformative experience. I stayed with a French family my parents had never met, I couldn't really speak their language, and their habits and customs were radically different to ours. During that trip, I made more progress in French than I ever have in my whole life, and I have never since had such an immersive cultural experience.

After my A levels, I spent another few months in France, and then went to university to read European Studies with French. There, I thrived academically, and enjoyed meeting people from different places and backgrounds and the freedom it gave me. It was another transformative and often happy experience, socially and educationally. We were treated like adults, and it was entirely up to us if we engaged with the course or not. Those of us who did were rewarded with good results, although there was no shame at all in finishing university with a 2.2 (lower-second-class) degree, as did many hard-working students. Loans were available to cover living expenses, but fees were still paid by the government, so there was far less graduate debt than today. I spent the third year of my degree course studying at university in Dijon. During this time, I mainly partied hard with other British students, but I also met a few French people who have become lifelong friends.

I stopped going to church during my university years, and I am not a churchgoer today, although a few of my old friends and some of my family members still are. I would still describe myself as culturally Christian, however, in terms of my moral framework, and I miss some of the elements that following a religious life meant – singing together in a congregation, collective ritual, and a tight-knit community. Our church included the wealthy and the poor, top professionals alongside the unemployed and homeless, people with stable lives alongside those whose worlds had fallen apart, people from all kinds of backgrounds and cultures, the old and the young, and many languages were spoken. Our church congregation was far more ethnically diverse than my school, because the Anglican and other faiths tend to bring disparate groups of people together.

University was a very positive experience for me, and I think it's for this reason that I made a career out of staying at university and never living in the 'real world' that had felt quite alienating when I was at school. While a graduate student, I met my now-husband, who trained as an academic historian and is today a freelance writer and curator. Our son was born in 2008, followed by a daughter in 2010. Soon after my son was born, I secured a position at the university where I now work.

I enjoy teaching students in their late teens and early twenties now, I think, because I identify with that life stage quite positively. Since my children were born, life has taken over. It has become a happy but busy cycle of work, children, family, home, chores and errands, visiting family, and holidays. I have always worked full-time; for financial reasons, we need one full-time salary. My husband builds his freelance work schedule around the children's school hours and holidays. He is a gentle, nurturing person and believes that raising children properly is one of the most important jobs that we do, and that the role of people who devote themselves to caring for children is undervalued in our society.

It struck me upon turning forty that by 2016, and in the few years that followed, I had suddenly ceased to be young. As a graduate student, I was young. As a first-time mother, I was young. When I secured a permanent academic job, at the age of thirty-six, I was still young. But the feeling changed in the years after thirty-five, when I felt forty approaching. Mary Ingham has written about facing the end of youth at the age of thirty, in the 1970s. We are living longer than ever, and marking the different life stages (finishing education, marriage and settling down, starting a family) around ten years later than most people did in the 1970s, when the majority of women left school at sixteen, after the national school leaving age had been raised from fifteen in 1972.[59]

Now I am forty-five, I am not young. My children have become teenagers, and soon enough, I will turn fifty. Perhaps I have less life left than I've already lived. With female friends, we are starting to talk about perimenopause. The years from forty to forty-five are an extraordinary turning point in life. At thirty-nine, you know it's perilously close. At forty, you know that your youth is in the past. But having approached midlife with a sense of dread, I find it a much happier life stage than youth, even though I must face the reality of my own decline and mortality. I feel freer than ever to enjoy life on my terms, and I care much less what other people think of me. Most of the people I have written about here echo this sentiment. It is now time to turn to their stories, those of the women with whom I shared the troubles and joys of my secondary-school years.

2

Anna

Anna lives with her husband and two young children in the London suburbs, a few miles from the place where we grew up. From the age of thirteen or fourteen, until the end of sixth form, we were close friends, spending most of our time together. Anna and I had similar interests in history, politics, reading, and travel, and we always felt comfortable in each other's company. Although we came from quite different families – mine was a large, well-educated but cash-poor family, and Anna was an only child in a well-off household – there were important similarities: our parents had been to university, and we both had grandparents who had been raised in working-class homes. Ours had become, in different ways, conventional middle-class families. Anna's parents took her out to restaurants and the theatre (and sometimes invited me too), and the family travelled all over the world, often accompanying her father on his summer research trips abroad. Anna graduated with a humanities degree in 1999, then trained as a lawyer. She now works in human rights advocacy for non-governmental organizations.

Anna begins by telling me about her parents.

'So my dad is a Geordie. He was a wartime child, born in December 1939, and he didn't know his dad for the first four years of his life because he was in a prisoner of war camp in Germany. He was in the merchant navy and was captured, and he was a prisoner of war entertainer – a piano player and accordionist. He got awards and things after the war, but when he came back, my dad didn't know him, and I think my dad had been very cossetted by women in the family. He had six aunts, and I think it was hard having a dad come back. He grew up in a council house, in an estate in South Shields.'

Anna's father had two much younger siblings, born after the war, and his father worked as a pilot on the River Tyne, guiding ships into port.

'My dad's the eldest boy, and he was a grammar-school boy, and first of his family to go to university. I seem to remember him saying that he did apply for Oxford or Cambridge, and was kind of a raw South Shields boy... and just didn't know how to navigate those kinds of ways but obviously was bright enough to get in. But he went to another university and studied sciences, and then did a PhD. Then he worked abroad for a couple of years, and then came back and met my mum. My mum is from a probably upper-working-class, lower-middle-class background. My mum is one of three girls, so she's the youngest and has two older sisters who are still alive, and I'm close to them.'

Anna's mother was from Devon, and Anna's maternal grandfather worked in the auction rooms. He was in the navy during the war, and Anna's mother was born in 1946, at the forefront of the post-war 'bulge' generation. She trained as a primary teacher and met her husband at the university where he was already working as a junior lecturer and researcher. Anna's father has had a successful career as a research scientist, becoming a professor and taking a chair at a London university while still in his thirties.

'I'm an only child and that didn't really bother me particularly as a child. I think it's interesting now as an adult, as a parent of siblings. I probably had a slightly different upbringing from other people... I had a lot more conversation and interaction with my parents at the meal table and on holiday. My dad was a scientist, still is a scientist, still working a bit, even though he's quite old now. My mum was a primary school teacher, but she didn't work a huge amount when I was small. I went to a small village school, and then a middle school, and then to quite a big secondary school.'

Quite early in our conversation, Anna mentions the fact that her parents separated for a few years.

'So my parents' marriage… it wasn't very apparent that anything was hugely wrong, but my parents did separate when I was eighteen, and they lived separately for some years but are now reconciled and living back together again. I think during my teenage years my dad wasn't around very much and that wasn't always very easy, but I have a good relationship with both my parents now. I think I noticed when I went to other people's houses that my parents' relationship was different, that we didn't talk about a lot of stuff, and that my dad was quite absent, but it still came as a massive shock to me, to find out that my parents' marriage was in difficulty.'

I ask Anna if she thinks her parents shielded her from their problems.

'Maybe, to a certain extent.'

Her parents had wanted more children but were not able to conceive again after she was born.

'So it was only when we were on holiday with another school friend in the South of France and I'd been caught out with a boy. I think it was only really at crisis points in my childhood that we had those frank conversations. I can't remember why it would come up after something like that, but that was when I discovered that my parents hadn't been able to have another child and my dad would have liked a son.'

Anna says she was close to her dad, but that he had very high expectations of her. This caused some friction between them.

'I was close to my dad, probably until I became a teenager, and then I think he just didn't know what to do with an obnoxious teenage girl. And he pushed me quite hard in some ways in that he would argue me down, as if I was an adult, which wasn't always very fair. It left me feeling powerless, I think. My dad was probably trying to push me to develop… and be more articulate and understand what I was arguing, but it was quite frustrating. It was quite isolating, as a child, to be argued down by an adult!'

At school, Anna was very academic and achieved top grades in all her subjects. I ask if she thinks her father had pushed her intellectually.

'I was driven, yeah... I don't necessarily regret it because I think if you are able to push yourself at school and you are successful, obviously that gives you greater opportunity later. I was having this conversation with someone the other day, wondering if my parents had had another child who was a boy whether my dad would have put a lot of the intellectual hope in him... I was the only one so everything got vested in me, and I think my dad had high expectations of me going into science, which I steadfastly didn't want to do, although I've kind of ended up with a career that is in a scientific area.'

Anna chose arts and humanities subjects at A level, like most of the girls we knew. 'I think once I could narrow it down to what I enjoyed studying, I think school was much easier to enjoy. I don't know whether it was because we had not very inspiring maths and science teachers... The quality of maths and science teaching at our school was... not brilliant. It was hard work to enjoy those subjects.'

Anna did stand out academically.

'I think I did feel different, because I was an only child, and because I was pushed quite a lot. I think, looking back, I probably came across as quite arrogant. As life's gone on, you get your corners knocked off a bit, and you... both soften and become more resilient.'

She doesn't think she was very aware of social class at the time, because everyone from all sorts of backgrounds had mixed at middle school. This changed when we started our GCSEs, and our different life destinies seemed to be sealed.

Anna agrees: 'I noticed a change at GCSE, and then again at A level. We were always in sets at school, and by A level it did feel like it was not as mixed as a school.'

Anna recalls the vocational diploma that pupils with four or five GCSEs could do at our school, instead of A levels. 'It was just in the lower sixth, wasn't it? It wasn't a two-year thing. But that divided people, didn't it? It split people, and there was suddenly the benefit of having had parents who'd been to university, who'd done it before... Also, I think there was an expectation from my parents that I'd go to university. And I think that wasn't necessarily the case for everyone.'

I ask Anna how she navigated adolescence and growing up.

'Gosh, really badly, yeah.'

Did her parents talk to her about it?

'No.'

Did school help with it?

'No. No one helped us. I would say that we had some friends who were quite sexually promiscuous from quite early, and that was a certain kind of pressure, though I think it was always quite clear that I was not gonna fall into anything that I wasn't comfortable with, but I think… I had a few encounters that looking back were a bit… unhealthy. That wasn't a normal thing to have done, to have gone off with a random man on a motorbike into the woods.'

I recall this incident, when Anna and a friend had shocked us all by hooking up with some bikers – fortunately, the one who took her into the woods was a decent young man who didn't pressurize Anna into anything and deposited her back home unscathed, although perhaps a little more experienced, by the end of the episode. Had she been led astray by Nadine – the rather outrageous friend she was with at the time?

'No! … The interesting thing is that Nadine was really shocked at me. That I'd taken the risk by pushing things further than she was perhaps willing to do.'

Anna's father was a scientist and an atheist who had once been a card-carrying Communist Party member (as very mildly radical young teenagers, we were breathtakingly excited by this fact) and whose views overshadowed her mother's more private Anglican faith. So when Anna unexpectedly converted to Christianity in her mid-teens, it came as a bit of a surprise to me – even though my father was an Anglican vicar, and I lived in a Christian household.

Anna says, 'I think I could've ended up on a different path if I hadn't become a Christian at fifteen. I think that was quite a defining moment, and it probably changed the way I related to boys and adolescence and whatever, and freaked my parents out completely… but it probably protected me from a route that might have been more promiscuous and confused and difficult.'

I suggest to Anna that, as young Christians, you're taught something different to what 'the world' (that is to say, mainstream society) teaches you about your body and what you should do with it.

Anna agrees: 'It's almost like a moral frame. And you kind of go... ooh, maybe that was a bit of a hard moral cage to put ourselves in. But it possibly did protect us a bit from things that might have been difficult. Having seen some of the relationships that people did form, that were quite abusive and difficult... I think, who knows, right?'

I ask if she thinks a lot of girls in our year were sexually active when we were young. It was certainly the stuff of rumours at school.

'I can remember those rumours of like weird, almost like orgies, like sexual activities at parties and stuff like that. And it was never necessarily the people in our class. I think probably from like fifteen, sixteen, there were a *lot* of people who were sexually active.'

But Anna thinks in our early teens there was a lot of talk and little action. 'It was probably less than we perceived at twelve or thirteen, and there was a lot of bravado. We had biology sex education, where we learnt about genital warts and stuff like that. And I feel there was a little bit in maybe either Personal and Social Education or Religious Studies or something like that, but it wasn't properly taught... it really wasn't.'

I managed to find a copy of a Christian pamphlet, *Girl into Woman*, on my older sister's shelf at home. It genuinely helped me to understand the physical side, but the guidance on the emotional side was much vaguer.

Anna agrees: 'That side was never, ever done properly. And I wonder if it still isn't. I don't know if it's shame or fear, or what. I don't know why people feel like they can't do that side of things properly. But you're right, it was very... it was quite biological. It just wasn't made normal, sexual development at all.'

I ask Anna if she thinks there was a big generational difference with our parents, or whether we were living in a permissive time. I didn't remember there being much shame in girls getting pregnant at fifteen or sixteen.

She disagrees: 'Gosh, do you not? I sort of feel like there was. It was shocking. I don't know how it would have felt, to be pregnant at that age at that time.'

But for a few girls, I suggest, it seemed *almost* to be a badge of honour, a marker of adulthood.

Anna says, 'I think there probably was that among some people, and I think that's still true now, actually, having overheard conversations on the bus!' She laughs. 'And I think, *Oh my goodness… you're thinking, this is just something to do, it's kind of quite exciting… but do you know how much your life is gonna shut down when you have to look after a baby, and actually give up your own childhood, your own youth… the times when you could be out just having fun?*'

I wonder if pregnancy and young motherhood enables certain girls to make the passage to maturity in a way that is entirely in line with their instincts. For us, the way we marked this transition was to get our A levels and go to university. But these young women, who were also responding to social cues and doing what felt natural to them, were forging their own path to adulthood.

Anna agrees this explanation is possible 'but not necessarily true for everyone. I think it's possibly not that thought through for everyone.'

We sleepwalked (in my case, quite literally…) through our A levels without thinking too much about where it was leading us.

Anna agrees with this: 'It was just what you did, right? I mean, yeah, definitely…'

Friendships were unstable in those early years of secondary school. Anna remembers me as a constant friend, although we grew closer later. She recalls, 'I obviously had some like… all over the place-ness in my first few years of being at secondary school. … I still had a friendship with Vicky, who had come up from my middle school.'

Vicky was a complex and fascinating character, but she was a tricky person to be friends with. Her parents were divorced, and – unusually for the time – she lived with her father and had a lot of responsibility for looking after the family, including

younger siblings. Vicky was easily a match for Anna intellectually, but by the time we got to our exams, Vicky had drifted into
another realm of influence. She was beautiful, so she attracted
the attention of the boys in the years above us, and they became
a distraction for her. Vicky dropped out of sixth form, already an
adult too young, and her life took a new and different direction,
although I think she did go to university later in life.

Anna says, 'You look back, and you think about your kids
having to go into that. And you just think, oh my word, how will
they survive? Because it is, it's hard, trying to find your place in
all that. I remember there being some big groups of people who
were quite intimidating. I can remember people shouting, like,
"Oh, that girl, I hate that girl," but, you know, in the scheme of
life, that's not proper bullying. That's a little bit of intimidation
in the corridors – that's not that bad.'

Anna is being generous, or diplomatic, in her description. I
found these girls absolutely menacing. We used to say they were
'hard', and they didn't shy away from ganging up on and beating
up other girls they didn't like. They had a kind of outlandish uniform, which included a thickly caked layer of foundation, heavy
eye make-up and shiny peach or pink lipstick – a hangover from
the 1980s – short hair that was slicked back with just a single
lock of hair pulled forward, combed down and gelled across the
forehead. In any other context, they would have looked faintly
ridiculous, but this was their domain, and they were the queens
of the school – and none of us were dressed much better, in
our baggy jumpers and big skirts, awkwardly concealing our
emerging curves.

Although the hard girls painted themselves in this way, the
hair and make-up was more tribal than an obviously sexual
statement at the time. There was something curiously masculine
about the girl-gang members. They wore big, shapeless sweat-
shirts instead of the regulation school polyester V-neck, opaque
black tights, and men's trainers. The school didn't strictly enforce
uniform rules. I am not sure what was really going on for those
girls, but it makes some sense now that if a child has a lot of
anger that it would swell during adolescence. But it wasn't very

nice being in their wider peer group, though perhaps if we'd got to know them a little they might not have seemed so threatening; their power certainly faded as we got older.

At the time, it felt deadly serious, but now it seems odd. How and why would a girl of thirteen be so full of aggression that she would just pick out people at random to attack? What was it in us that she found so threatening, and why did *she* seem so completely fearless? It was as though she had to puff herself up like a cockerel and assert her dominance in the meaningless hierarchy of the school.

Anna recalls, 'There were fights in that bloomin' rec [recreation ground] out the back. That's kind of shocking. I don't know if the fights were willing… Were there people who were willingly meeting to fight, or was someone goaded into it and felt really frightened?'

To me, these girl-fights seemed slightly staged – although the violence was not fake. They were highly orchestrated events, and every person in the year seemed to know when one was scheduled to take place, and one specific girl was often the aggressor. The victim was always terrified. Yet none of us ever dared tell the teachers what was going to happen. Perhaps we wanted to see the thrilling denouement of the pent-up tension, or perhaps we were scared we'd get found out and beaten up too. There was a strong unspoken code of not grassing, not telling, and the teachers were always left to mop up afterwards.

I have no idea how many of these catfights were intercepted by teachers beforehand. There was something qualitatively different with boys' fighting – it seemed more spontaneous and quickly forgotten, whereas the girls' fights were planned and surrounded by ritual and mythology, and designed to send a message to everyone about who was top dog. This generally hostile environment didn't make those early years of secondary school very happy for many of us.

Anna says, 'I was not very happy… and for me becoming a Christian at the age I was, it was quite a transforming thing, and I think it did make a huge difference, and I also think it gave me a sort of club – and identity. I became a Christian into a church that had quite a lot of young people in it, at a time when there was a revival movement going on. There was quite a lot happening, it felt quite exciting.

'I definitely felt there was an inner transformation, but I also probably benefitted from suddenly having an identity and being part of a bigger group and circle. It didn't stop me having boyfriends! It was almost like an advent of boyfriends! That's when I started going out with people! People who were slightly older than me. It was an opportunity to meet different people, maybe, from being at school. But it also gave me a measure of control.'

The environment Anna and I inhabited as older teenagers, in terms of the church, was one in which we were unambiguously taught that sex belonged only within marriage. Not everyone stayed within these parameters, but some young people took the guidelines seriously. Although such restrictions could be stifling, for Anna and me it provided a safe set of boundaries within which to experiment.

After we finished our A levels, Anna took a year out and went to Latin America for six months to work in a children's home. Her desire to do altruistic work and to make the world better, to work towards social justice, has been there for as long as I have known her. Although I thought it was courageous of her to go to live in another continent on her own at nineteen, Anna doesn't think so.

'I think it was very stupid! It was suddenly where my overconfidence and gung-ho attitude got grounded in reality.'

She had no experience of working with children and couldn't really speak any Spanish – although she learnt on the job: 'It was a formative experience in teaching me what I did not know…'

These days, young people on a year abroad are often actively discouraged from working in orphanages. Many organizations will not work with them anymore, because it is recognized that family-based care, where possible, is preferable to institutionalization for children's psychological development.[60] Anna is keen to stress that the place where she worked was a children's home, with a big extended family setting and not an institutional orphanage. Nevertheless, I can tell it makes Anna cringe a little, thinking back to her former self, with what she calls her 'white saviour' mentality – one that comes quite naturally to a young person first faced with the injustices of the world: 'I think my perception, my understanding, of justice... it's incredibly different even from five years ago.'

Anna went on to read American Studies at university, which included a year abroad in Mexico.

'I enjoyed university a lot; I loved it... I made some close friends; I loved my subject. I have really fond memories of it. I was mainly single and not particularly promiscuous, but I just really enjoyed the sociability of it, the intellectual interest. There's something I suspect about university then, that was you were treated like an adult – it was like "you get what you put in".'

Universities in the 2020s are different. In 1994–95, we started university in a low-risk but high-potential environment. Today, I think my own students feel under pressure to achieve a certain result because of the high fees they pay but also because we, university teachers and staff, treat them more like children. The stakes are much higher, for staff and students. In the 1990s, we paid no fees, and many of us could claim a maintenance grant. This meant that university was affordable to everyone with a small loan or a part-time job. University management was not the slick bureaucracy that exists today, and the idea of the 'student experience' had not yet been invented – we were taught by the best academic specialists in their respective fields, and the libraries were world class, but resources were otherwise modest, and the buildings were sometimes run-down.

The social side of university life was as important, and often just as enriching, as the academic side. Everything from a pint in the student union bar, to lunch in the vegetarian café, to renting a shared house was cheap – your money went a long way.

Anna is gifted academically, focused, and endowed with good judgement, so anything she set her mind to in life was possible.

'I trained as a lawyer because I wanted to work in human rights. As a child I always hated injustice, I hated poverty, I had a lot of very good intentions, I probably had a white woman saviour complex, which meant I thought I could go and help.

Looking back, I feel quite squeamish about that. I feel a bit mortified. I wanted to do human rights law because I wanted to help people. I do still want to change the world, but the means by which I believe the world is changed, and the agency of people and things like that, is very different from what I might have thought then. I feel there's something... very middle class and white and patronizing about the way that I perceived change... how you build movements, how you work with people who are different from you, the fact that some struggles are not your struggle. I think it is a justice and finance and resourcing issue, in that we hold so many of the resources. I think movements should be grassroots, and should be empowered, and should be supported, and should be linked and brought together.'

Anna has worked for several large non-governmental organizations and charities based in and around London, and currently focuses on climate justice. She works with grassroots associations across the world to campaign with communities that will be most immediately and directly affected by climate change. It is community based, but she does feel that the charity has to employ certain strategies to keep the funds coming in: 'Some of the fundraising, the ways that you get money to places, almost has to be through making white people feel good about themselves. So that's hard... really, really hard.'

Anna got married a few years after finishing university.

'So I felt that I was quite behind everyone else, which is absurd because I got married at twenty-seven. There was a wave of church friends getting married before, during and after university... at twenty-one, twenty-two. But I feel pleased that I got married that little bit later, and I think I had some relatively unsuccessful relationships. Either I went out with people who I was quite intellectually compatible with, but we possibly didn't share a faith or a world view... or I went out with nice people who I didn't feel very intellectually or politically compatible with. I think meeting James was the first time that it felt much more of a... meeting of minds, someone who was clever and interesting, and different from me in some ways, but we had a lot in common, we could do a lot together... we had shared politics and faiths, so I think it felt very, very different. We got married in 2003, and we have two children.'

Having their two children was not a straightforward process for Anna and James. I am aware when raising the subject that it was not easy for her.

'No, it was not. I try to be quite open about this, because I feel like it's not always openly discussed, and it's very painful for some people, and I'm not worried by being open about it. I think I was someone who was never that bothered about having children… but I think hitting thirty-one-ish, maybe towards thirty-two… and a lot of our friends were having children, and we thought… we're ready, let's go for it. And then, of course, it just didn't happen and didn't happen.'

In the UK, if you have issues with fertility, you wait a year before the NHS will begin the process of investigating.

'It looked like I had low progesterone but everything else was more or less alright, and they said, "You can have IVF in two years, if you still haven't conceived, but the likelihood is that you'll conceive in that time…" So we tried for another two years, bringing it up to three years, and it's… it's incredibly painful, watching everyone around you conceive and have children, and some people having two children or more in the time when you've been trying to have one, and it's obviously… It's challenging for your own, like, your sex life, your relationship, those kinds of things, because it becomes something that you do in order to try and conceive rather than just because you want to! Becomes a bit of a burden, you know… it changes a lot of things.

'When I look back, I think those extra years gave me time to progress further in my career. I don't think I'd have been able to pick up my career after children as easily as I have because I had three and a half, four more years of actual work experience, and we travelled a huge amount, we did lots of interesting things, and although it always felt like second best at the time… at the time we'd rather have had kids. But I think if you'd told us in advance that we would have had kids further down the line, we'd have enjoyed it a lot more! But I look back and I think… we did all that train travel all over Europe, and we went there, and we got the train to Morocco, and we did a road trip in Ethiopia.'

But Anna still did not get pregnant.

'We sort of hit the three-year point, and then got the referral… and then my periods disappeared completely, and all the things we needed to test for a certain day of my cycle in order to get our referral… they completely disappeared, and in the meantime, I agreed to go part-time. I decided that I wanted to go part-time, because although I loved my career, I felt like it was time to take a choice that maybe would help me.'

Eventually Anna and James were able to get the referral they needed and had IVF within six weeks.

'We were incredibly fortunate in that I got pregnant on the first round of IVF, which was amazing. I don't think I believed that I was actually going to have a child until he was born alive and well. I feared the whole time that something terrible would happen, and one of my very close friends had a still birth at thirty-two weeks, and it just felt like it was so… it felt so fragile. So it was quite an amazing thing for us. To have a child, and we didn't know whether we would have any more, and, you know, one – the difference between zero and one is the difference. You might yearn for a second child, but it's not… it's not the same as the sadness and grief of not having a child.'

I suggest to Anna that once you cross the threshold of having a child, if you have had to wait, you can no longer fully understand the pain of not having any. Anna has travelled much further down that road than me, so she tries to keep the feeling close.

'I always try to have huge empathy with anyone who's experiencing infertility because of how traumatic and difficult it is – I never want to forget how difficult it is. But I understand that I have crossed a threshold. And that however well-meaning my sympathy, empathy, whatever is, I don't know what it's like to never know if you're going to have a child anymore.'

I ask Anna how it was for her mother to become a grandmother.

'I think our parents were just so thrilled. Because I'm an only child on my side. And on James's side, his brother was also experiencing fertility problems, so… it brought huge joy to the grandparents. And I still feel like my son is really cherished by the three remaining grandparents… as the firstborn of the grandchildren.'

Neither getting pregnant, nor being pregnant, nor giving birth was easy for Anna.

'I had a terrible birth, absolutely dreadful. I had a back-to-back delivery, I had a third-degree tear… it was awful, and quite traumatic. I don't think I expected to have a traumatic birth. So that was a bit of a shocker. And I think it's a massive shock, having a newborn baby, it's such a huge adjustment, and it was incredibly hard. But I also think the fact that I'd waited for so long… I felt more ready and grateful for that kind of collapse of normal life. My mum has looked after both my kids from quite early on, and there hasn't been any conflict interestingly. It's maybe partly not having siblings, but it's partly… we just have a really close mother–daughter relationship. Sometimes we rile each other, but I feel very comfortable with her.'

How does her mother's life compare to her own, in terms of equality, opportunities, and so on? I say that we were supposed to be the generation to achieve complete equality, and Anna quickly replies, 'Yeah, which we don't at all.' She feels that she and her husband James have an equal relationship. But Anna does not think they are typical.

'I feel like I've suddenly looked around – and this has probably changed in the last five or six years – and I feel like most of the women I know no longer work, and are married to people who are the main earners, and do all the childcare, and I am a bit like, "At what point did I turn around and wake up in that era of traditional marriages?"'

Anna believes these women give up work because they still face barriers in the workplace.

'I think some of them, literally, their workplaces would not allow them to work part-time. So there was an actual barrier. It was either you come back completely full-time, you work all the hours, or you've got nothing. I'm surprised by how many people experienced that, and I find that disturbing. I've been incredibly fortunate, because I've changed jobs twice since having children, and I think that's unusual – to get two part-time jobs in your field is something that doesn't happen very frequently. I just see a lot of really gifted, talented women, where there's been no option for them to do a role in a part-time capacity, and that makes me really cross. I still feel we have a workplace that is essentially designed to suit men. It's not designed to be flexible, to allow people to work part-time, to share jobs…'

I am always looking for mentors in my own job as an academic, so I often ask women older than me how they forged a path. There are a few patterns. Many of the senior professors I know are women who do not have children, or women who are independently wealthy. Childless/child-free women have more time and energy to devote to their research, and often progress quickly. The wealthier ones are able to buy time by employing nannies and housekeepers and cleaners and other types of 'help'. Some of these women take unpaid leave, or long career breaks, or they can afford to work on a fractional contract – all effective strategies for gaining time (albeit unpaid) to progress writing projects, which lead to promotion.

Many women advance more quickly once their children are much older – well beyond primary school. A few of the female academics I most admire did not start publishing until later in life. The esteemed philosopher Mary Midgely published her first book when she was in her late fifties and went on to publish twenty books. She never reached the rank of professor because she retired before becoming a prolific writer, but she was a world-class academic.

Children need to be cared for properly, and the conclusion I have reached is that it's better to accept this and find a way of balancing family life with job responsibilities that works for you. This is more constructive than comparing yourself to people who have made other choices and might have different resources available to them.

Anna adds, 'I also think there is a slight element of choice in that I'm not as senior as I could be, and part of that is I really hate middle management. There's a level of stress and internal politics and stuff that you have to do. I'm choosing to do something I'm really interested in. And it looks counter-intuitive because I'm not paid as well, and I took a pay cut to take this job, but I'm doing something interesting that I really enjoy, and I need not to feel stressed about the fact that I'm not as senior as I could be. If I'd chosen things differently and arranged my life differently, I possibly could be in a more senior position, but I'm not sure I'd be happier for it.'

Some feminists have concluded that the workplace is not only structurally but also psychologically set up to reward men.[61] It is structured hierarchically and rewards ambitious people who actively seek promotion through its ranks. I have friends and colleagues who are able and high-flying, but who after having children found they just couldn't combine motherhood with a pressurized career. The rewards were few, and they felt they'd proved themselves – they'd published a highly rated book, they'd secured a permanent academic post at a top institution, but there were also other things to which they wanted to devote their lives. But should women seek to emulate men, and is female success to be measured in terms of what society sees as success for men, or should women be seeking a different idea of what makes life meaningful?

Other feminist thinkers, however, would rail against the suggestion that women should accept mediocrity or a different standard of excellence to men.[62] Women who are child-free by choice, for example, would likely disagree that those who compete effectively in the public sphere and modern workplace are simply aping male behaviour; this idea suggests that ambitious women without children are somehow not 'real' women. The argument follows that restructuring the workplace to suit *mothers* is not necessarily in the interest of all women.

Anna pauses as we both reflect on what we might have achieved professionally had we been childless.

'I think I feel relatively content, and I'm slightly annoyed with myself for being content about those things. I am happily married, in a good relationship with someone who I feel like… we will be together as long as we live. You don't know what the future holds in terms of your health, but we are a strong partnership – it's not a perfect partnership and we still have arguments, and we still get it wrong, but I feel content within that... we do make each other happy, and, having struggled to have children, I do have two children. I take a great joy in that, and I also take joy in doing a job that I love and find meaningful and interesting. I don't think it's that common to have everything together, and you don't know how things will go in the future, but I think it made it easier, turning forty.'

Anna is pleased that she was able to make the move from the law into social justice advocacy.

'It does give me great joy to work in – even though it's a depressing area to work on climate change at the moment. It's completely horrific, but this is the fight I want to be in. And if it doesn't work, you still have to fight for it, because it's the right thing to do, and you go down fighting.'

I ask Anna what she thinks are the main issues facing women today. She feels (aside from the global existential threat of climate catastrophe) that it relates primarily to combining family and career.

'I see a lot of women struggling with their identity because they haven't necessarily been able to carry on an area of work that they've been good at, and that they've loved. While they're probably fantastic parents, they probably struggle with being at home with their kids the whole time, because I do. It's not what I'm naturally good at. It's much harder than going out to work. It's hard finding your identity in that. I see women who probably feel like they've lost their identity a bit, and they've lost who they were, because they don't have any place in which they are just... who they are. I'm relieved that I have an identity in a place where I am who I am still. And a lot of women don't have that anymore, and I think that's quite tricky, because men do tend to have... if they're still the worker... they have a place where they're not just a dad.'

Anna sees a lot of women start careers that they have to abandon, because the flexibility is just not there.

'I see a lot of women going back into little jobs. Bits and bobs, to fill the time and bring a little bit of extra money in.'

Anna doesn't look down on women who organize their lives or time in this way – it just doesn't seem to her that they have any other choice, and that's hard. It seems to be a feature of living in the Home Counties, where so many men commute into London to work long hours in highly paid jobs. There's little opportunity for women to continue their careers part-time. It is all or nothing.

She says, 'If you've been successful in an area, or good at something, or something's made you really come alive, to not be able to do that anymore... I just think that's a real shame.

'I see a real mix around me, but I see far more women not working than working. And far more men who do the kind of jobs that are completely all-consuming, and pay for everything, and they are never around. I think the further you get out of London, and the more you get into perhaps a more alternative kind of place, there might be far more balance. It might be that I'm seeing quite an extreme here.'

In the university city where I live, it does seem to be more balanced. A lot of people here work in education or in hospitals, and although there are more stay-at-home mums than dads, many men have prioritized family life over career. My own husband, who started out in academia but left to work as a freelance writer and curator, says that he has aimed, in his own life, to break down ideas of what a successful life should mean for a man – that children and family life might be as good a measure of 'success' as a traditional career.

But many women in the UK experience what Anna has observed, and what Rebecca Asher also describes in her 2012 book, *Shattered*:

> Despite our now quite determined efforts to share the parenting equally, a combination of habit, social structures, cultural norms and cold hard earning power means that I have become, and remain, the foundation parent. [...] In the midst of my own early shock and disorientation, I realized that the abrupt divide that my husband and I were experiencing was being replicated all around me. My exchanges

with other parents in playgrounds and baby clinics signalled that ours was part of a wider story.[63]

For Asher, the prevailing expectation that women are the primary carers of children, often even after they return to work full-time, is what breaks many women. It is the reason that Anna sees women dropping out of careers because they simply cannot split themselves between two such important roles in a way that their husbands and partners never have to.[64]

Anna travels to the office on the outskirts of London, about half an hour by train, one or two days per week. Her role involves international travel, and she is fortunate to have parents and in-laws who live nearby to help with the school run. But the costs of childcare are still a strain.

'I have a lot of help, and so I have huge advantages. And I mean, we're absolutely flippin' skint with childcare... we're desperate for when Molly [Anna's youngest child, who is three] gets her childcare paid, because that will suddenly free up £600 a month. And we're finishing every month £600 down, so frankly, that would just about bring us back into balance!'

Anna is, like several of the women I've had conversations with, into running.

'I only started doing it this January. I'm one of those people who, my weight fluctuates a bit, but I'm relatively slim. But I read some stuff about people in their late thirties and forties who are sedentary and drink a lot, and eat well, and... who basically drink a ton of wine at home, which is what we do all the time! And they're a ticking health time bomb. A lot of us are likely to experience having looked reasonably fit and well in our thirties and forties but may well experience quite severe health problems later in life. I felt a bit like, no, I'd like to take care of myself a bit better. I'd like to lose weight, which hasn't necessarily happened with running at all, but I'd like to feel a bit fitter... in better condition. But I also feel the gym is not a very practical option for parents, because there is a lot of faffing about, and it's quite expensive. Whereas I think running is something that, I mean, I do it as part of a group... I pay a termly fee, and we run together, and so there's a social element to it, but it's something you can do for free. If you ever got to the point where you can't afford to do a running club, you can still just run. You can do it wherever you go in the world, pretty much.'

The beauty of running is its simplicity. You just put on your running shoes and go out the front door. And sport is one of those rare social activities that acts as a leveller, where we meet people of other ethnicities, and where social classes mix. I ask how it makes Anna feel when she runs.

'I really like it. And do you know what? I'm still a really, really fast sprinter. I'm faster than everyone! I was fast at middle school. I love running fast. It's one of those things where possibly, if I'd trained, and pursued it as a young person, I could've got better.'

She's pleased to rediscover it now, on her own terms, and without the competition of school.

How does Anna see the world for her daughter? She is understandably pessimistic.

'I feel quite afraid for both my children. Because I work on climate change, and I know how bad things are, and whenever my colleagues and I talk about it, we're just a bit like… we shouldn't have kids.'

I am quite shocked to hear Anna say this, and there is a hesitancy in her voice when she does. But it's understandable when you consider she is faced daily with the reality of a situation most of us can ignore.

'It's really frightening, and you always live in slight semidenial, and then you get added layers, like the economic suicide of Brexit… and all the horrors of that, and what that potentially entails in terms of the world that our kids will grow up in. I feel like, in some ways, Brexit was… like ripping a mask off. I thought we were in a very different place as a country from where we were. I thought that we were progressive, I thought that people were quite liberated. Not so prejudiced, not racist… It makes you see your country quite differently.'

It's important to Anna that her children see her working.

'I think there was a study that said that boys whose mums work are much more likely to grow up and share domestic chores. And girls whose mums work are much more likely to have a career. And… there's no hard and fast rules about these things. But I think… I want my kids to feel equal and… not that they can do *anything*, but I want them to have lots of choice, about who they are and what they become. But I want them to understand, also, injustice and poverty… to see that people live differently, that we are in a privileged bubble here, and that is not how most of the world live.'

Anna and I wonder, in our conversation, if we are living at a moment of high cultural decadence. I sometimes feel like we're living in another European belle époque… that period of relative peace, prosperity, and the dominance of progressive or permissive (depending on your outlook) ideas before the carnage of the First World War and the rise of fascism in Europe. That we are living in this moment of unsustainable privilege, but that it's a fragile status quo.

I ask Anna how she feels about the current debates and feelings running high among young people over questions of sexuality, gender, and identity. She thinks her children seem to have relatively binary identities at the moment.

'I don't know, you have to cross those bridges with your kids. I feel far less rigid and concerned about that than I think I maybe would've done in the past.'

I suggest this is a result of growing older and just seeing the world for what it is, in all its complexity.

'It is… and also just going, gosh, let's not tie ourselves in horrible knots about something that's kind of, like, loving someone…'

Anna does not want to dwell too much on it, and her answer is clear – live and let live. Not that she is uncomfortable with it, but that she does not want to put pressure on her children in terms of gender roles, and she wants to see how things evolve for them. She is aware of the process of gendering children, which she wants to avoid: 'I try and treat my kids the same.' She doesn't like it when people buy her daughter dolls.

'I try to buy quite non-gendered toys, and hand down Toby's toys. Why would I go out and buy her a fairy, you know?'

But Anna recognizes it is still more complicated than this. She and I both still buy dresses and skirts for our daughters.

'It's not just about dressing your daughter in pink! It's more subtle than that. And I still feel like I'm a part of that gendering, and I don't know how to fix that…'

3

_____

Kate

Kate rents her home from the local housing trust. It's a modern – 1970s, '80s perhaps – detached, three-bedroom house in a cul-de-sac punctuated with mature trees, in an affluent commuter village that runs into another small town, both gradually absorbed into the fringes of London. A single mother, she still lives a few miles away from our old high school, which her three daughters also attended. It's the type of house that many British families live in, but this row of houses is modest within its wider surroundings. In this town, footballers' wives can be spotted in the local Waitrose, or shielded behind the darkened screens of their SUVs. There is huge wealth here, but not everyone has money. Kate works hard and has always provided for her family, but earning a living has often been a struggle. Her eldest was born when Kate was nineteen. Her now eighteen-year-old middle child sits in on the conversation with us, half listening, half scrolling on her phone. Sometimes she nods or smiles in agreement or recognition, and sometimes she joins the conversation.

Kate's adult life has been marked by a sort of precarious stability. The security has been provided by her, as the anchor to her young family, now in their late teens and early twenties. Kate grew up in the area, in a nearby village, to parents she portrays as loving but immature and irresponsible 'hippies' of the sixties counterculture, although the bitterness she once felt about the early abandonment she experienced has gradually dissipated.

Kate's parents had met when they were still in their late teens, in the early 1970s. They met down the pub, which, as touched on earlier, was a culturally important meeting space for young working people for several generations in the UK, from the 1960s to the late 1990s, before the age of social media and the general decline of pubs that began in the late 2000s following the ban on smoking in public.[65] Whether you were on the dole, jobbing, careering, at sixth form or university, Friday night was always pub night.

'My dad was from the States and he was drafted to the Vietnam War when he was nineteen, and he wouldn't go, and because his parents had emigrated when he was two, he had a British passport. So he was able to come out of the country, unlike his friends, who had to go to war; he met my mum and within six months they were married! I think it was in part to do with that, and also, they had this whirlwind romance. I have no doubt they were in love – they both said they were.

'My dad married my mum a few years before I was born. My sister was born first, and then it was me eighteen months later. When I was two and a half, my mum and dad separated. My dad stayed with us and my mum moved out for a year. My dad had custody of us. Then, when I was about four, just as I'd started school, my dad decided that my mum would be better off with us. She had met someone else, and they were a bit more of a stable influence. My dad moved back to the States… and then we didn't see him until I think I was about sixteen. We wrote letters and things, but it wasn't a relationship as such. So my mum and stepdad brought us up until we moved out, pretty much.'

Kate's mother found that the rock 'n' roll lifestyle she'd been drawn to in the late 1960s had ill-prepared her for the two small babies that arrived in the mid-1970s. She was left feeling stifled, unable to cope with the drag of parenting.

'He was a musician, and my mum was artistic, and they both took lots of drugs. Having children, to them, was like the "whoa!" sort of moment! Because me and my sister came along, and my mum couldn't conform… she really couldn't. I think that's why she walked away, because she could not conform to

2.4 children, living on a council estate and suddenly having to step up. She wasn't ready to do it at twenty, twenty-one, because she had a very hedonistic sort of lifestyle. And my nan often said, "I was constantly having problems with having to rein her in."

'We lived in a council house. It was a brand-new estate, so it was lovely for us, great for my mum and dad. That's why they could be flexible with the housing situation. My mum could come back and carry on bringing us up, and my dad moved out. Mum was a stay-at-home mum until we were about eight or nine, and then she had sort of shop jobs really – I think she worked in a little kitchen shop, and then in a card shop, but it was all part-time to fit in with school hours, and my dad – my stepdad – by trade was an electrician. So, yeah, it was quite comfortable. We struggled a little bit, but it was generally a nice sort of upbringing. We had friends on the estate that were similar ages and that we ended up at school with, and all their parents had similar jobs. It was generally a stay-at-home mum and dad went out to work. And then Mum worked full-time from when we were eleven or twelve. I think she started off as a secretary, and then went on to be a personal assistant to a managing director of a company, so ended up with a really good job. Dad was self-employed at that point; he was doing really well, so then we started having nice holidays and things, and life was a bit better from probably about eleven, twelve.'

Kate has had time to think through the repercussions of her parents' life decisions, and for a long time directed her anger at her father, the more obviously abandoning parent.

'We would call each other a couple of times a year. I didn't have that great a relationship with my dad, because I always harboured that kind of "you left us", you know? More so that I did my mum, which is a bit strange. I don't know why, but I think because my mum came back and realized she'd made a mistake, I made allowances for that, and she was a pretty good mum bringing us up. She did do the right thing.

'I used to have my yearly conversation with him on my birthday, and I'd say, "Why are you ringing me up on my birthday?

All you're gonna do is ruin it… because you don't ring me up any other time of the year, and then you choose my birthday, and then I have to have a go at you, because you're such a shit dad!"'

Kate simply felt, 'You left us, you should've stayed, you could've, you didn't.'

On one occasion, when Kate was still at primary school, her father visited England. He turned up at the school gates, but Kate refused to speak to him. 'My sister did, and I thought that was really treacherous of her, to do that!'

But as Kate grew older, she found herself able to help construct the emotional bridge her father was trying to build. Starting with a trip to the US when she was sixteen, paid for by their father, during which Kate and her sister 'spent the first two weeks not talking to him', the relationship grew again. Kate wanted to punish her father, but found herself starting to talk to him and discovered she 'really liked his personality', and in her thirties had a 'moment' when she decided to forgive him, saying, 'I've got to let go of this now, this is not good for my mental health, I have to let go of all this anger towards him.'

Kate's feelings flipped from those of an angry adolescent to a responsible daughter at the time her father became ill with cancer. He returned to the UK to be cared for in a local hospice until his death in 2000, when he was still only in his fifties.

Kate's stepfather appears in the family story as a stabilizing influence. Kate called him 'dad', and he remained committed to the family, to his stepdaughters, even in later years after he had separated from Kate's mother. I ask her if it feels like he's her dad.

'Yeah, so I'd see him, and he'd pop round. He'd always spend Christmas with us, and I've probably been closer to him than either of my parents.'

Kate uses 'dad' interchangeably to talk about her father and her stepfather. They both fulfil this role for her, in different ways. Kate's stepfather was the person whose unconditional love enabled her mum to be a mother again: 'I mean, my mum wasn't a natural mum… my mum left me and my sister when we were little, and she came back because my stepdad encouraged her to come back and be a mum, and my dad [Kate's biological father] I think was probably relieved. I always think I've got a lot... I owe a lot to my stepdad, because he held our family together, and he helped my mum to bring us up.'

For Kate, moral ties, the feelings of attachment and sense that you should do the right thing are stronger bonds than biological connections. Kate's stepdad didn't have his own biological children, but Kate and her sister were the children he decided to raise.

Kate enjoyed school for the social element.

'I liked it, because I had my friends there, and that was the most important thing. Not so much the learning side, but the friends side – the fact that you're with your friends all day and you can enjoy the time you spend there. I loved English, and I loved history, but I'm not academic, so even though I loved it, I struggled, and I tried really hard, but I still just got Cs in English. I got a B in history, but that's down to my history teacher, after every lesson in GCSE, saying, "Right, now we're going to spend twenty minutes together, and I'm gonna go through the whole lesson with you," and he did that throughout the whole of year eleven, pretty much.'

Kate is artistically talented (you can tell by the stunning garden constructions she produces out of nothing but wooden pallets and a tin of leftover paint), and she wishes that the art teaching had been better, more passionate. Instead, many of our teachers were jaded from years working in a comprehensive school. But Kate feels, overall, grateful for the schooling we were given.

'I think I was probably given the opportunities, but it's like I always say to the girls: it's up to you to take it, and it's up to you to pursue it. You have to do that; you can't expect them to keep putting out for you if you're not gonna take the opportunities you're given.'

Still, I can't help but feel that Kate, aside from a few exceptionally supportive teachers, had fewer real opportunities than she supposes – educationally, socially, and emotionally. Kate left school with five good GCSEs, the benchmark then for being able to 'do something with your life', and went to a local college to study a BTEC vocational qualification in Art and Design.[66] She was interested and engaged at first, but like so many young people, especially in the affluent South East, she was tempted away from education by the promise of a weekly pay packet.

Talking about college, she says, 'I really enjoyed the first year, loved the first year... By that point I'd got a job in Tesco. They were opening a big store nearby, so we all went over there in September, and I think that was where I made my group of friends, and then my social life was that. College-wise, there were a couple of friends, but no one I really clicked with, and so by the second year, I was just getting through. I just wasn't enjoying the subject particularly. I think I was all arted out! I applied for university. I was gonna go to Winchester University, and I was all geared up to go, and then they offered me a supervisor's job at Tesco. So I went "okay then" and took that because of the money, and I didn't go to university.'

Kate could talk to her mum about puberty and growing up.

'I was probably ten, I remember my mum having a conversation with my sister in the kitchen about periods and your body changing, and it was very much, "This is gonna happen to you, and when it does, it's absolutely fine – it's what all women go through." But when it came to sex and relationships, there was very little in terms of information and conversation. Sex-wise? No, no, it was friends. We talked about it as friends: "Oh, who's done it, who do you think's done it, who's gonna do it first?" You know, all those sorts of conversations. I remember looking at a book – my friend had a book!'

We all laugh at the idea of children learning about sex from books, but it was the only objective source of information we had. School was limited to biology.

'No, no guidance as far as relationships go, or how you're gonna feel emotionally.'

Kate's daughter, despite growing up in the era of the internet and social media, says it has not improved much since our day.

When I interview Kate, my children, who were born when I was in my early thirties, are still quite young – under the age of ten. Kate's three daughters are already almost grown up. Her eldest has left home, and her youngest is nearly at the end of compulsory schooling. The closeness she has with her girls is a striking effect of being closer to them in age – they are not quite a generation apart. Kate was only just an adult when she had her first daughter, and her middle daughter's presence in our conversation suggests an intimacy and honesty that I am not sure I will share with my own daughter, who is three decades younger than me.

Kate's first pregnancy was unplanned, but it was also something she embraced wholeheartedly. Her relationship with her daughters' father began soon after leaving school.

'I was eighteen and he was twenty-six. He wasn't working at the time; I don't know what I saw in him! I started moving in with him within a year of meeting him, and then I worked in a coffee shop in the village as assistant manager. I did that for a while, and then that's when I got pregnant with Ella. I was nineteen then, twenty when she came along. It was something completely unplanned. I did work the dates out many years ago, and it was the week we moved into the flat together. That was a real life change, from the moment I got pregnant. Because our lives – mine and Chris's, and all of our friends' lives – consisted of getting through the day job to go down the pub. That was our lives – literally! At eighteen, nineteen years old, it was. The highlight of the day was getting your uniform off and going down the pub. And seeing your mates, having a good time, looking forward to the weekend, looking forward to payday, you know… So no, we didn't think ahead at all. None of us thought ahead! None of us actually thought, *What are we gonna do with our lives?* We were just in the moment and having such a good time. I do know that those were some of the best years of my life.

'And it's not that having children stopped my life – it changed my life; it didn't stop my life. So Chris and I were living in a flat. It was a maisonette, there was a couple downstairs – they were all our friends as well, so it was a bit of a party house – and we shared that for pretty much the nine months of my pregnancy, and I stayed there until I think probably days before I had Ella.

We couldn't take on the flat by ourselves, because we couldn't afford to.

'We went to the council and said, "We need to be housed," and they said, "No, we won't be housing you because you've got an income and you don't qualify… you can privately rent," but we couldn't afford to because we were broke, so I went back home to live with my mum… and then I got a place by myself, and then Chris moved in with me. And that was basically what the council told us to do. And that was the only way that I was gonna get a place.

'So we lived in a halfway house. Well, I did – I wasn't allowed to have Chris there, so I lived there by myself with Ella for four months, which wasn't too bad actually – it was okay. It wasn't the worst sort of place to live.'

I asked Kate how it felt to have her family broken up in this way, when she had just had a baby.

'I think, I was so in love with her – I know it sounds daft, but I was so in love with her at the time – she was my world!'

The thought brings Kate to tears.

'When she came along, she was just everything to me.'

What we don't often think about, or what governments don't seem to consider when enacting punitive policies against much-maligned 'teenage mothers' – who are often people like Kate, acting without thinking ahead, living in a carefree way, and loving and caring for their children – is the psychological impact of insecurity. Kate speaks frankly about her fears and about the feeling – a deep rumbling suspicion that she wasn't trusted to do the very thing she was doing so well.

'It didn't matter where we were, as long as I had her, and I think at one point I thought, *Oh God, what if she gets taken from me*? So I was quite protective as well.'

This part of the conversation, where Kate recalls her fears about her child being taken from her by social services, is probably the most difficult. Her face is strained as she speaks.

'I did think I would be questioned because I didn't have a home. But I had confidence in the fact that I was a good mum, and I knew I was. I knew I was from the day I had her, so I didn't worry about that, but there was that "I haven't got a home, so I need to provide a home for her", and Chris had his own issues. By that point he had depression quite badly, because he'd been a big drug user throughout his life, and I put quite a lot of pressure on him to give up drugs, because I wasn't a drug-taker, but he was.'

Kate knew she couldn't tolerate it anymore, now that her boyfriend was a father, telling him, "'You've got to give this up; this can't be a way of life anymore… this is something you've got to knock on the head…" which he found hard – he knew he needed to, but he found it hard to stop.'

To Kate's mind, Chris's drug problem stemmed from a very difficult upbringing, and a family history of serious psychiatric illness. She seems partly to feel compassion towards him for this, and partly to see it as a weakness to be avoided.

'I think there was a lot of hereditary things in him as well. Again, that's what I've always said to the girls, you know, "Think about the partner that you choose, and think about character traits," but it's easy to say that in hindsight as a forty-year-old woman that's had those experiences and lived with people.'

Kate's natural warmth and openness meant that, like her mother, she followed her heart where she urges her daughters to follow their heads. Like her mother had met her father, Kate also met Chris, the father of her own children, down the pub.

'At eighteen, I fell in love with a man who I thought was amazing. That's it.' At the time, she felt, 'He was the love of my life.' And despite the problems Kate has described, the young couple were able to rise to the responsibility of looking after young children.

I ask her what the advantages were to having a baby young. She says that she was able to be young with them, and to be an energetic mum.

'I definitely had the energy to be able to do everything and anything. We were quite spontaneous as well… we'd just go out for the day and get on a bus, get on a train, pack up, have a picnic, and off we'd go.'

Kate stepped easily into mothering. Women in their thirties and forties having babies seem to need instruction manuals, but

Kate thinks that women in their teens and twenties tend to just get on with it without thinking too hard.

'I didn't think about too many risks… and now, working as a nursery teacher, I am far more aware of risks. I was very naïve as a young mum, but I do think that worked in my favour. My kids were never sick. A classic example is, I went into hospital to have Ella, and when I was having contractions, they said to me, "How are you going to feed your baby?" and I said, "What do you mean?" Because I'd never been to any antenatal classes. So I hadn't talked about, you know, breast or bottle feed; it just hadn't occurred to me, and that's so naïve to think that, because now, if I was having a baby, I'd have it planned, I'd have everything planned, but with Ella, I didn't think about it, so when they gave her to me, I went [Kate gestures as if cradling a newborn baby and lifting it to her breast]. And that was normal, natural, perfect! It was instinctive, to just go, "Oh!" and it worked for all of them!'

Kate didn't have any expectations about what a baby should or should not do, which made the whole process smooth and natural for her.

'Not that I didn't take seriously their health and their existence. I did. They were my world – all of them were my absolute world, you know.'

Mothering was a spontaneous process for her, where her own mother's strongest instinct had been to run away. It's here that you wonder if the example of unconditional love and devotion that Kate knew from her stepfather is significant. But Kate is magnanimous towards her mother and seems to understand that, although it came naturally to her, it might not have done to someone else. She has forgiven her mother, because she came back and cared for her family even when she did not initially feel the same bond or attachment as Kate had with her children.

One of the ongoing struggles in Kate's life has been housing.

'So we're under a housing trust scheme, but I've got a long-term tenancy, so I've got certain securities, but with changes in government, you never know what's gonna change.'

She had to be officially single and homeless before being eligible for housing with her first baby, despite always having worked and never failing to pay her rent. With two more children in tow, the family needed something bigger.

'I was pregnant, and we were in a two-bedroom flat. It was tiny, so I'd already said to the council, "We need something bigger, so, hopefully, if you can find something bigger for us, that would be great."'

Meanwhile, Kate was combing adverts for council house swaps and found a woman looking to downsize: 'She came round and had a look at it and she said, "I absolutely love it. Do you want to come and see my house?" and I said, "No, if you like this and say yes, then I'll come and see your house," because I was eight months pregnant by that point, and I thought, *I can't bear the disappointment if she says no!*'

It turned out that the woman did want to take her flat.

'So we came over here and we had a look at it, and I just burst into tears! I mean, it was ropey, it had old carpet and was completely dated, but it was just, "Wow, this is perfect!"'

For Kate, decent social housing enabled her to build a secure family life. Her youngest daughter has lived her whole life in the same house.

'It's affordable living – we're lucky to have it. These days I think you've literally got to be living on the street with five children to get a house. Any sort of social housing. It's such a dire, dire situation.'

And without council provision, buying a property is out of the question.

'This house up the road has just gone for about £420,000, and you just can't relate. It's just ridiculous… The income that you would have to be on to afford this house is just crazy.'

Following the house-price booms that happened in the mid-1980s, early 1990s and early 2000s, property prices in London and the Home Counties, and in many other parts of the country, are now so high as to be completely out of reach for many younger people on low to middle incomes.[67] To buy the modest family home rented by Kate today, you would need to have saved a deposit of 5 per cent, or around £20,000, and your monthly mortgage payment would be in excess of £1,700, even on a relatively low interest rate. Those with a combined household income below £60,000 need not apply. The median household income in 2020 in the UK was £29,900.[68]

After they were housed, Kate and her partner experienced the familiar juggle of working life and managing young children.

'I got housed, then Chris moved straight in with me. By this point he had got a job working as a tree surgeon, and then I worked part-time at Tesco's, when Ella was about five months old. I did evening shifts, so I'd drop her to mum-in-law's, because she was just round the corner. I say mum-in-law's – we weren't ever married. And then she'd look after Ella until Chris got home. He'd collect her and bring her back, and then I'd be home from work at about ten o'clock in the evening; that was three or four nights a week. So that was okay.

'I breastfed all of them – I breastfed her for six months, so that was a bit tricky, organizing that before I went out. And then Ava was planned. I wanted another baby straight away, because I think you just go on your own life, don't you, and I was so close to my sister, and I thought, *Oh, and I want that gap*, so that they've got a sibling.'

Kate's sister had left England to go and live in the US with their father, and has lived over there ever since. Coincidentally, Kate fell pregnant with her second child at the same time as her sister. But this time, Kate lost the baby.

'So, I was pregnant, and I was out with my nan, we were doing some shopping, and I suddenly had a massive bleed in the middle of the shop, and my nan knew what it was straight away. And she took me home, and that night I miscarried, so that was… that hit me quite hard, that was a real shock, but as I generally do, with anything in my life, I just got up and went to work the following day. Forgot about it – didn't forget about it, but just got on with it.'

Kate is very positive about the experience of pregnancy.

'That hit me quite hard, but I never had, you know, postnatal depression. I was lucky… All my pregnancies were really good. I loved being pregnant, absolutely loved being pregnant… it was the best feeling – again, [addressing her daughter] we were just talking about this the other day, weren't we? It was the most amazing experience… absolutely loved it when they were little. I got pregnant pretty much straight away after that and had Ava.'

Kate continued to work day and evening shifts while looking after her two small children, with the support of her family.

'I was doing evening work still, then I was working in a toy shop, during the week for a couple of days. … By this point, Ella had started nursery, so they used to let me bring Ava into the toy shop with me in her little carrier! She used to sit behind the desk while I got on and worked. So that happened for a few months. That couldn't be carried on, but my employers were great! They were a really old couple and were just like, "Yeah, bring her along!"'

With the baby growing and starting to move around, Kate couldn't continue doing this job so she took evening work again, this time in a local branch of Waitrose. Then, to her surprise, she fell pregnant again.

'I got pregnant with Sophie when I think Ava was about eleven months old, which was a complete shock!' She laughs. 'I'm not sure how I got pregnant – so irresponsible! So irresponsible! Oh my gosh, looking back on my life, honestly! Just learn from my mistakes, Ava!'

Her daughter, who is listening, finds this funny – but Kate assures me that none of her daughters are in a hurry to have a baby.

Kate's mother, like her father, died relatively young, at fifty. I don't ask how she died, and Kate doesn't tell me what happened. I respect this, and in some ways it doesn't matter. But Kate does talk about the decade before her death, and the gradual unravelling of her mother's life, which was clearly linked to her untimely death. Kate knew her mum and dad had experimented with drugs in the 1960s and early '70s. Although her mother managed to stay clean during Kate's early childhood, she started using again, and drinking heavily, in her thirties and forties.

'She snorted quite a bit of coke when she was in her younger years. I think I was about sixteen, and I was with my sister, and we were in the living room, and I pulled out something from under the sofa, and it was a piece of glass with a razor blade on it, and my sister said, "That's to draw a line up." Because I didn't know that at sixteen, you know? I knew she'd had a past, because she'd told us she had a past. But then I think she'd got quite a bit of a habit, certainly when I'd just had my first daughter Ella, because she gave up a really good job, and she had a bit of a breakdown. She was working for a company, and she was personal assistant to a managing director, so she had a really good job. It was well paid, she had a fantastic clothing allowance, and she was dressing up smart to go to work every day.'

Four men who worked at the same company as Kate's mother were posted out to Saudi Arabia to set up a new telecommunications system.

'They went missing while they were there, and then there was news that they… It was horrific, but their heads had been found. They'd been beheaded out in Saudi Arabia. And they were friends of my mum's, friends of all the people in the company. They had families and children, and it was horrific – really, really horrific. I remember my mum dealing with that when Ella was a baby. My mum couldn't cope with it at all, and I think she started using then, and that was the point that Mum and Dad were having marital problems… they had completely separated by the time Ava came along in 1997.'

The issues Kate's mum had with drugs and alcohol meant that, despite the love between them, their relationship had a certain necessary distance. They lived a few miles from each other, but Kate didn't see her often: 'I suppose we used to see her three times a year maybe?'

Her mother demonstrated the tragic unreliability of an addict who is falling apart, but trying to save face, to keep up appearances.

'I remember going round there one time… and she'd made us a chicken salad, and I cut open the chicken, and I'd given it to all the kids, and it was raw, and I went, "Mum, the chicken's raw!" and she was like, "No, no, no, it's not raw!" and I gave it back to her, and I was just like, "Oh my God, oh, Jesus Christ!"'

Kate's mother died soon after this incident, when Kate was in her early thirties.

Kate's relationship with Chris did not last beyond her children's teens, and she finally broke up with him six years before our conversation. His instability meant that Kate found herself alone as a parent as the girls grew up, isolated from friends since moving away from the village where she'd grown up to move to the new house. Chris had got the family into debt through credit-card spending, leaving her feeling stuck.

'It was probably, in some ways... the best time, but in some ways it was the worst time because I'd chosen to move there. I had to get the bus every day to get Ella to school and it was exhausting, so it was quite tough, and he wasn't much of a support. He loved the girls, and still does love them, but he just wasn't supportive. Emotionally he was draining and exhausting. By that point, I just couldn't cope with his depression as well as dealing with the girls – it was just too much. I look at photos of myself then, and there's a lot I don't really remember. I think we were hanging in there, because I just wanted to keep our family together.'

Since the break-up the girls have stayed with Kate.

'They've always lived with me, and he floated around for a bit; he never had a permanent home. Nowhere that you could go and visit and spend time with him.'

I ask Kate how she feels about turning forty, and how it is to be a mother of teenage girls today. Kate is emphatic that having children, although not planned as such at the age of nineteen, was a good thing: 'It changed my life; it didn't stop my life.' But she is still wistful about the fun and freedom she enjoyed before children came along, before the permanent, low-level parental anxiety started.

'You have to have those times; you've got to have good times. You've got to be careful – I think there's far more danger now.'

I press Kate on what she thinks is more dangerous now, and she feels the world has changed in certain respects since we were at school in the 1990s, since the wave of immigration from Eastern Europe that occurred during the Blair years in the 2000s.

'It's things like, well, cultural differences. I know when Ava's off to clubs, and, you know, it's not just English guys at the club anymore, it's European… and further afield, and they have different ways of thinking about women.'

Perhaps because of her exposure to drug use as a young woman, Kate worries about her daughters being tempted into it.

'And that's my worry. The drugs. I think there's so many more drugs these days; I think there's far more than was about when we were kids. I think there was the standard coke and speed, and a bit of marijuana, and a few pills, but now, there's so much.'

Kate worries about what can be purchased over the internet, and where these drugs come from, and what's in them. She feels we've departed from a world where people knew what drugs were, to one in which we have no idea what they are. The effects of drug use on her own life have been quite destructive, but somehow this enemy was a familiar one. Perhaps it is just the future, and the unknown, that is frightening.

Kate wishes that mental-health issues were better addressed in school.

'Ella went through a tough time when she was fifteen, and the mental-health support, it's diabolical. The best help she got was from a youth support worker who went into school unpaid, you know? I think there is a lot put on teachers to have to deal with these things, and they're trying to teach their subjects as well.'

Kate thinks that our generation, growing up in the 1980s and '90s, had fewer social pressures than today's teenagers.

'The internet's huge… just a massive influence. It's not necessarily a good one. There's no switch off, you know? Like, with bullying for example, when Ella was going through a horrible stage at school, she'd come home and there'd be texts on her phone, and she'd open up her phone at eleven o'clock at night. I know when my sister was being bullied, her safe haven was home, and she didn't have to think about it or worry about it.'

Money has always been tight for Kate, and she has often been in debt, so she wishes our education had been more practical and geared towards dealing with everyday life. I agree wholeheartedly and tell Kate that I wish I'd been taught how to plumb in a washing machine, but her point is a more serious one about the purpose of education and training.

'We never had lessons on how to budget... on what we needed to pay as adults... on mortgages, rent, insurance. If you got that in school, then you'd think more about being an adult, but when all you're being told is you need to go to university, go to college, get a job... you need to actually focus it on "the reason you need to get these qualifications is because you will be having to pay rent, you will be having to pay an electric bill and a gas bill", and do you ever remember being told those sorts of things?'

But it's a constant struggle to make ends meet.

'Inflation has gone way past wage increase, so we're losing in that respect. I've had this conversation with my dad, and with my uncle, and they're both tradesmen, and they are both on the same wage now that they were on in the early 1990s. Ultimately, of course, happiness, that's what you want, but I do think you have to be financially secure too. We've always managed to afford to live, but we've mainly been in debt... you need to be able to live to your means; you need to be able to pay your rent every month... to be secure financially.'

Kate, who currently holds down two jobs, still works as hard as ever. Her daughters also all work part-time.

'I'm the assistant manager of the nursery... term time, I do about twenty-five to twenty-eight hours for the care company, and then I do twenty for the nursery.'

She has a little more time in the holidays, but this regime is intense and unrelenting, and does not allow her much time to be with the daughters she is still bringing up.

'It's too much... its draining, and it just takes up so much time. I just haven't seen the girls for the last two years.'

Because her punishing schedule doesn't allow any time to socialize, Kate tentatively decided to start internet dating when she felt ready to meet someone new.

'I went on a couple of disastrous dates, and then I met Jon, and yeah, he's lovely! He's an actor, he's very different from someone I would normally have gone out with – he's not my type at all, but he is a really nice man. He's from up north and he's an actor!'

It is still early days with the new relationship, but Kate feels supported, and that she has found someone who is the opposite of Chris, her first love, in a good way.

'I'm probably the happiest that I've been for a long time now,' Kate reflects.

Jon is keen to get married, but Kate is not in a hurry. She says that he'd like children but will 'settle for a dog'!

We conclude our conversation with another reflection on family. Kate says that she's looking forward to her daughters having their own families.

'You know, now I've had them, they've made my life, and I say to them, "I'd love you to go to university, I want you to have the experience, I want you to go and travel, and see the world, and do all those things." I didn't go to university, I probably should have, but ultimately, you know, what made me the happiest in my life was being a mother. It's not defined me, but it's certainly made me the happiest.'

She has tears in her eyes as she says this. We all end up crying a bit. This is what matters most to Kate, in the end.

4

Emily

I meet Emily in May 2017, at a local branch of Costa Coffee, in a modern shopping centre in the suburban commuter town where she now lives, just a few miles away from where we grew up. It's twenty-five years since we left school, and therefore twenty-five years since we've last seen each other. We were in the same tutor group, so saw each other daily for four or five years, and then, all of a sudden, never again. I suppose we didn't reflect much on it at the time, but there is a complicity between classmates created through regular, familiar contact and the common experience of school and going through adolescence. I think this recognition of an old friend is why, instinctively, we enthusiastically embrace as soon as we see each other.

I ask Emily first about her family, growing up, and the place where she is from.

'I grew up in a council estate in C—., which is quite a nice area, but obviously the estate wasn't so wealthy, and it was quite an interesting place to grow up, because that estate was new. It was built, and then everyone who moved into it – they were three-bedroom houses, so there had to be two children – and there was suddenly a whole council estate populated with children my age, or two or three years younger. There was a park outside my house. I didn't spend so much time in my family home, but a lot of time out the front playing, with probably a group of up to twenty children at a time. And all my life, I've thought that was a good thing, and it was a lot of the time. More recently, when I've reflected on it, I've realized that actually it was probably a bit... I don't want to say feral. We were just left out there, and the socializing was quite harsh. I was probably dealing with social politics much earlier than a lot of children have to, and not really sheltered from it. You couldn't just go home and ignore it. It was there all the time, so I had quite a nice childhood, but now, I realize it was much tougher than I thought it was.'

Emily grew up with her mum and dad at home and a brother who is two years older.

'I had quite a stable and happy upbringing. We went on holiday to Cornwall every summer. And then my parents divorced when I was about thirteen, fourteen, and that was quite difficult. It had quite a catalytic effect on my life – a big impact on my teenage years.'

Emily didn't get on with her brother.

'He's quite severely dyslexic, and in those days, they didn't really understand dyslexia, or couldn't diagnose it, so he spent a lot of his life thinking he's not very clever, when actually he's quite bright. But he couldn't read. He was put into a lot of the remedial groups at school, but he was clever enough to know that he wasn't clever, which I think was quite difficult for him, and I think he might have resented me, because I was quite bright. He always felt like I could read and write, and everything was quite easy for me.'

I ask Emily how she felt going up to our secondary school, and about our educational experience there.

'It was quite scary. In our primary school we had two classes – there were sixty children in a year – and then to go to that school, which was huge, and not know your way around... we had to have a map, and it felt quite restricted. It wasn't like people were just running around doing whatever, but it did feel like I was quite vulnerable. I think the education was fine. I don't think it was great.'

Our school, being an average state school on a council estate, but also situated in an affluent wider area, drew in a mixture of children from all social backgrounds up to the middle classes.

Although it lacked the upper classes and wealthier upper-middle classes, the school created an environment in which we mixed and got to know people with lives different to our own.

Emily says, 'What school did do for me was introduce me to a demographic outside of my area. When I grew up, to be honest, my parents didn't really mind what I did. They had no aspirations for me to go to university or college. They weren't thinking much past me just having dinner. They never said to me, "What are you going to do when you're older? Are you going to university?" I never had those conversations.

'My mum wanted me to pass exams, but she hadn't really thought past what would happen when I had my exams. I've got a daughter now, and it's like, "Well, okay, so these are your strengths. What will you do? What career could you have? How could we help you?" I don't think my parents thought about that. I think they just… looked after my physical needs, and my immediate emotions, without strategizing about what I might do when I was older.'

Emily thinks that meeting other pupils like me and Anna, whose parents had been to university, opened up possibilities for her and made her more ambitious. This is interesting to hear, because my feeling about school was that it slightly deflated our levels of ambition, but clearly we had internalized the parental expectation to succeed in higher education – to the extent that it also rubbed off on our peers.

Emily says, 'I think at school, I met people like you and Anna, who had clearly different guidance from their parents, so you had ideas about, "Well, I'll go here and do this," and that never occurred to me, so I do think that made a difference.'

Emily's family and mine might in fact have been in similar situations financially – dependent on child benefits, and neither was a home owner. Holidays were camping or caravanning (borrowing someone else's) in Devon or Cornwall. But Emily was right to intuit that my family was different to hers, in terms of social and intellectual capital – both my parents had been to university in an era in which most people did not go on to higher education. Even though my parents' attitude to our education was fairly hands off, there was an underlying expectation that we would go to university – which all four of us did. Compared to today, very few people thought hard about 'what they were going to do in life'. Going to university was a risk-free milestone; it was free, and it was a stepping stone to other things. Then, there was much less of a 'squeezed middle' in global macroeconomic terms, and less competition from developing nations and outsourcing, which today tends to lead to a laser-like focus on education and social mobility for the children of aspirational parents.

In our generation there were a small number of people who were very driven to achieve something in particular – to study medicine, or law, to get to Oxford or Cambridge, or to get rich or become a successful artist of some kind – but for many of us, higher education was just what you did. Emily did not share this assumption, but meeting people at school whom she describes as this 'different demographic' planted a seed in her mind that would only bear fruit later in her life.

This shift can happen in a generation. My grandparents didn't go to university. Emily's children will likely go on to higher education, and those raised expectations are firmly in place. Emily's father was an electrician and, before that, a postman. Her mother was a secretary and also ran a cleaning business. Emily used to help her mother clean pubs and restaurants when she was a child. Her parents were hard-working, and resourceful, and they passed on this work ethic to their daughter.

Emily was a bright pupil, but she left school at fifteen.

'So I got five A to Cs. It was fine.'

Emily had achieved enough to move on to further education, rather than directly into low-paid work, but it didn't work out for her right away.

'I tried to get into college to do my A levels twice, but by that point I was involved in drugs. I was smoking a lot of weed. My parents divorced when I was fourteen. I was going out with a guy who was eighteen, who was older than me. So my mum left the house, and it was just me and my dad, and my dad didn't cope very well. He basically just lay down on the sofa – it's really

sad! – for about five months. So I went through this period of...
I thought I was quite resourceful, looking after myself. When,
actually, I probably wasn't looking after myself. Then I got in
trouble.'

Emily was, like me, an August baby, and we both finished
compulsory schooling at fifteen, in the summer of 1992. I spent
a month of that summer living with a family in France, preparing to start my A levels, and the rest of it doing pot wash
in a local restaurant for £3.20 an hour. Emily, cut adrift by her
parents' divorce and lower educational expectations, spent the
summer smoking dope.

'I really damaged myself, psychologically, that year.'

Emily's progressive slide into drug use stopped her education.

'It got to the point, when it came to September, I just
couldn't go to college. I was too nervous and too paranoid to go
out of my house... My mum had to come, and she was totally
bemused, like, "What's wrong with you? You were this confident
child, and now you don't even want to go to college."'

Emily got a couple of cleaning jobs, which was about all she
could manage alongside her chaotic lifestyle.

'I still used to smoke a lot of weed. I could do quite low-level
jobs until I was about eighteen.'

She had a job at the Hilton, a large local commercial hotel.

'I was like, "Well, I can't do this forever..." I knew I was too
bright to work as a chambermaid at the Hilton forever, so then I
learnt to type and got a job as an office junior. Then I worked up
to an admin assistant. And that was when I was about nineteen,
and I got thrown out of my house when I was nineteen, which
is a whole other story, so I went to live on my own in a bedsit.
When I was nineteen, I was an administrator, and then I got a
job for a software company, working on the support desk, and
then I just worked my way up from there, so I stayed in that
industry. So now I'm a project manager.'

Emily didn't do any post-GCSE qualifications until 2012,
when she was thirty-six.

'I started to look to get other jobs, and the jobs I was apply-
ing for, which were over about £50,000, they just expected a

degree of education that I didn't have. Then I took a part-time degree in business. I had Olivia in 2006, so she was six.'

My impression when we were at school had been that Emily was intellectually underdeveloped – that we were all, to some extent, regarded with benign indifference, but that she and many like her were overlooked and subject to low expectations. I wondered if sometimes decisions were made about people based on their perceived social class. Emily says that this sense of not being entitled to succeed still exists.

'For a long time, before I did my degree, I would be at work, in business meetings, and I would always feel like – they call it the imposter syndrome, don't they? "I'm in a group of intelligent people, and I don't know why I'm here! They'll know that I'm from a council estate, and I'm actually not that bright. I don't know what I'm doing here!"'

At this point, mentors and female supporters became important in Emily's life. When her children were young, Emily became friends with another woman from a similar background. This made Emily think about some of her beliefs about what she deserved and could achieve.

'When you grow up on a council estate, there's a working-class thing… you have a level you shouldn't really go past. So we're always like, "Well, I work really hard because I have to, and… I couldn't have this, because that's not what we do. Like I wouldn't have a four-bedroom house, and I wouldn't do this and this."'

But Emily's friend challenged her on this, saying, 'Well, why wouldn't you? You're taught to work as hard as you can, and do the best that you can, and you're pleased for anything that you get. Whereas middle-class people are taught that they deserve everything.'

Emily had to move away from this way of thinking to advance career-wise.

'That psychology is quite an important thing to break, and I probably only did that in the last seven years.'

I ask Emily what she thinks made her able to make this break, and she puts it down to a drive to make money, to achieve financial security – all driven by feelings of insecurity.

'I know now, because I've recently had counselling about it. I was really driven, but I wasn't necessarily driven for the right reasons. I had a very difficult time in my teenage years, and when I was nineteen, and I remember living in a bedsit, I was earning £9,000 a year as an admin assistant, and I thought, *Do you know what, no one's gonna help me here. I have to do this on my own. I have no money, I can't afford to eat, I have to get the bus. I have to do something.* So I was very driven to get money. For me, there's a big issue around security and money. Then I was driven. Not through the greater drive to expand yourself, to get knowledge, and grow, but driven by… almost fear. So through a lot of my life, I was going for two jobs, always looking to change job, to earn more money, to make successful appraisals and get pay rises.'

Emily's story reminds me of one of Mary Ingham's interviewees, a girl who had felt the weight of poor expectations from teachers:

Even those who didn't get into university had begun to cut their ambitious teeth. Shirley had always been aware of her working-class background at school: 'But at the time I had this feeling, I'll show them one day. The headmistress told me I wasn't university material, which made me more determined than ever, so I decided to resit one A level and did some student teaching in the meantime. When I got into university, I was quite a different person. I went armed with confidence and also this determination that people weren't going to stand in my way; that was all behind me.'[69]

This anxiety about financial security remained until Emily had her first child, in her late twenties – a little later than most of her childhood friends, who had started families in their late teens or early twenties. But starting a family made Emily rethink her motivations.

'When I had my children, which probably isn't a surprise, then I was like, "Okay, why am I doing this? Do I still need to earn more money?" But I still didn't feel very entitled, until I did that degree. So my friend Cathy said, "Well, if you do that degree, you'll realize that degrees aren't that hard! And you just think, because no one in your family went to university, you think there's this barrier, and that these people are different from you, but they're not different from you." She almost had to tell me that. I think a lot of people with the same background as me aren't as driven, because they are not as scared of having nothing. I had to, because no one was gonna give me anything.'

Emily has thought a lot about all this over the last few years. She thinks things might have been different for her if her parents had been more aware.

'I'm much more socially intelligent and emotionally intelligent than I am, I think, academically intelligent. But even if my parents had been able to handle the divorce differently and been slightly more nurturing and supportive... I would've felt more able to do A levels, and then even to go to university – I think my life would've been very different if I had, because then I would've moved out of that demographic. My mum did try in this respect, but she had left the family home, and my dad was struggling to cope as he'd recently been made redundant.'

Clearly, in a sense, Emily does now have the life she envisages in this hypothetical scenario. She has moved into the professional classes, and her own children will probably go to university. This life has arrived a little later than it might have done, and perhaps she would have been even more successful, or made more money if she'd realized it earlier. But she has remained connected to her origins: 'I'm still friends with those people that I grew up with on that council estate... some of them are my best friends.' We might move demographic, as she says, but we often come from the same places, and there are important commonalities to our life experiences.

Emily remembers adolescence as an isolating time.

'I had a lot of people around me. But no one that really understood who I was or what I was doing, so I felt lonely for a lot of my teenage years.'

She could rely on her friends to be around her but didn't have anyone to talk to about difficult things. I wonder if we do, as children, still rely a lot on parents at this stage – and Emily's were unavailable, overwhelmed by the breakdown of their own relationship. Consequently, Emily felt unprepared for adolescence and sexual relationships. She had her first sexual experience at a young age, with a local boy, and 'was completely unprepared for it'. Emily says it's sad that her parents didn't talk to her about it, in the way she talks to her own daughter.

'At ten, she's already come to me and talked to me about how people get pregnant, so I've had a conversation with her about – this is a strange way to say it – but about how men can be a little bit predatory. I've had to say to her, you have to be careful with how you manage yourself, and don't give yourself away too easily… You need to be emotionally ready for it… because I didn't expect to be rejected. I just thought, why wouldn't someone like me? Why wouldn't this be okay? And then when I was rejected, it was awful.'

Emily's mother didn't know about this immature relationship, nor the rejection Emily experienced after taking things too far, too soon. Later, Emily started going out with another boy when she was fifteen, and he was nineteen.

'So my mum did talk about that, and first of all she said that I shouldn't, obviously shouldn't be sexually active, because it's not legal!'

Emily is laughing telling me this – the question of legality seems preposterous, when it was already happening.

'So she was quite angry at first – she actually went to the doctor and complained. I went to the doctor and went on the pill, and my mum went to the doctor and complained to the doctor that he'd put me on the pill. And then he said, "Mrs Smith, would you rather that I just let her get pregnant?" After that, we had quite an open understanding about that – that I was in a relationship where I was having sex, but that was quite difficult for her. What she didn't do, which she probably should've done but maybe didn't know how to, was she didn't teach me early enough about the fact that… you have to be emotionally developed enough to put yourself in those relationships.'

But how does a parent teach a child, who is by nature immature, of the importance of maturity?

Emily wonders why we all felt that it was all or nothing in relationships – that if you went out with someone, it meant you were supposed to have sex.

'It seems interesting that nobody spoke to me and said, "Oh, you can go out with boys and not have sex."'

This lack of dialogue meant we lacked a language with which to talk about sex and relationships, and we lacked agency and control over our lives and bodies – at least, the only way of having control was to abstain or check out, like I did, or to go all in, like Emily. Neither was very healthy.

Emily sought stability in the relationship with her teenage boyfriend, during the period her parents were divorcing, but her boyfriend could be violent.

'I was going somewhere I shouldn't have been going for emotional support. So I was with him till I was twenty-one. That was so bad… I was in a pub once, and we were watching football, and he hit me in front of people.'

It wasn't uncommon for our peers to have their first sexual experiences in their early teens. How does Emily think this was handled by our wider community, and indeed society?

She laughs. 'Oh, I just think they pretended it wasn't happening! Do you remember our sex education, in that block? And it was one or two lessons, and it just covered the physical side, and no emotional side. Even my daughter, at ten, has had a better sex education. There was a whole thing lacking. I've got a theory about this… we weren't taught to regulate or look after ourselves inside, so we were taught to physically look after ourselves, like, "Yeah, you've got to study and eat," but no one ever said, "You need to look after your emotional well-being."'

Emily thinks that this lack of emotional attentiveness has its roots in our grandparents' experiences of the Second World War, and how that was lived by our parents' generation.

'I think it's to do with the war – their parents were in the war, and then they came back, and they just must've been completely emotionally all over the place… "You're just lucky – they're lucky to be alive…"'

Emily's own grandfather, who had been a sniper in the British Army serving behind enemy lines during the war, was psychologically damaged by the experience of having unintentionally harmed civilians who were caught in the crossfire. His trauma, and haunting guilt, had an impact on Emily's mother, who had 'quite an emotionally stunted upbringing'. Emily thinks this emotional repression continued for us as the generation that followed: 'I think our children will be the first generation of children after that war that will have proper emotional guidance.'

Emily's grandfather took to drinking when he came home from the war.

'And my grandma would… they spent their whole life almost protecting him, so it was almost like, "Don't make Daddy argue," and treading on eggshells around him.'

This heightened tension was transferred onto the whole family and affected his children the most.

'I thought he was a nice and kind man, but my mum spent all of her life feeling that she couldn't be herself.'

We talk some more about school, and our adolescence, and our preparation for life. I ask Emily if she thinks there was any shame in relation to teen pregnancy or if it was expected?

'I think there was a bit of shame attached to that. I think they felt ashamed. Not because of the baby; I think it was just because we knew that they shouldn't have been having sex. So it's like, "Clearly you've been caught doing something that you're really not meant to do!" I don't think I looked down on them, but also… they could have been aspiring to more. That said, if you have children that young, you'd probably be quite resourceful afterwards.'

Emily says a bit of her feels like it was a waste of a young life, but she isn't sure. As she says, people have second chances in life, and who are we to judge when the right time is to have a baby?

Emily got married at twenty-two, which she feels is very young. She and her husband were in love but got married young because he is South African and would otherwise have needed a visa to stay in the UK. They have been married over seventeen years.

'I was only single, which was probably not great, for three years, so— and that is a fault in myself, in that I needed, I'd always needed someone quite close. As almost a bit of a leaning post. Me and my husband split up for three months in 2015, which led me to evaluate a lot of the stuff that I have done in my life, and which is why it's probably easier for me to talk about some of these things. We got back together, but I needed to do that, to check I was happy in the marriage and in it for the right reasons.'

Emily needed the break to reassess the life she had chosen.

She says that they're much better off than her parents ever were.

'In the last year, we bought a four-bedroom house. I've got an en suite… I've got a car; I've got an Audi. My husband's got a car, I've got an au pair – she drives an old Zafira. My life is completely different.'

We joke about the three cars and the suburban stereotypes.

She laughs. 'I am a suburban mum!'

I ask Emily if she thinks her children will go to a school like ours.

She answers emphatically, 'No. We don't earn enough money for me to send both my children to private school, but what I've been lucky in is that I sent Olivia to a free school, which is run by a woman who went to Oxford and studied the disparity between state and private school. And she believes that you can give independent schooling within the funding that you get from the council. She believes that you can teach children that they are entitled to more, that they can succeed. Their slogan is "Optimum Omnibus", which means "the best for all".'

The theme of ambition and bettering yourself runs deep in Emily's story and it's what she wants to pass on to her children. She has been deliberate in her schooling choices for her daughter, where others have been more accidental in their approach, so that her children 'can be taken to a school where they're nurtured and really taught that they can be whatever they want to be. And that they can just assume they'll go to university, and they're… I suppose exposed to some of those areas in life that I just never was.'

Emily says starting secondary school opened up a new world to her, in terms of what she saw and how other people's lives were.

'I was in a council estate, and I never knew anyone that was much wealthier until I went to senior school. And then that was probably you and Anna.'

It's interesting to me that Emily perceived me as well off. My father was a vicar, and my mother didn't work (though she had been to university). With four children to feed and clothe and a large draughty vicarage to heat and maintain, my parents had little spare money when I was growing up – although they were noticeably better off in my later teens and twenties, after my mother went back to work. But Emily was right to perceive the difference, as she had already noted, in the limited sense of social class – most clearly manifested in the unspoken expectation that we, as children, would or would not go to university.

In Emily's case, this was just something that other people did. She hopes her children's schooling, along with the example she has set in achieving a degree later in life, will break the cycle of low social-class expectations.

'I think if your children believe that they can be successful, they can probably be successful. I think the drive to be successful is much more than being clever. You have very clever people who aren't driven to want to succeed... that's okay too! As long as you've got the money to survive.'

I ask Emily if she feels there is a lot of academic pressure on children nowadays. She thinks there is, but that it might always have been that way for middle-class children.

'My dad just obviously thought I'd grow up and get married and have children... I genuinely don't think it occurred to him that I would do more than that.'

For her own children, she tries not to let them get too worried about SATs and other exams.

'I'm strong enough in myself that my children aren't impacted by that, which might be wrong, because they might be too relaxed, but because I've done a lot of drugs, came from a difficult background, and I've worked up, I don't really care what people think, and I'm pretty sure my children don't care either. I don't feel that I need to conform to any of society's norms.'

I ask Emily about turning forty, and how it feels for her. Is it a good age to be, as a woman, today? She sees starkly the bleak side of it first.

'It's a bit depressing! When you're forty, you're definitely on the other side of young. You might be closer to the end of your life than the beginning. So that's quite scary. I'm reluctant to let go. In some ways, I'm quite immature in that sort of thinking. I'm sure at some point I'm meant to grow up! I shouldn't be drinking wine till three in the morning! I shouldn't be scooting down the road, but I'm still doing that stuff, so I wonder… when am I gonna make this mental transition to be a grown-up? And I don't want to be making it!'

Most people seem to report that forty is a better age to be than twenty-one.

She agrees: 'I'm much more experienced and more happy in myself, and I think I was happy with myself then, but through ignorance.'

I want to ask Emily about running, which is quite a preoccupation among middle-aged women – including me.

'So why did I start running? I've always been slightly overweight, which I do worry about. When I had Ethan, I was fifteen stone. I was really quite overweight, so I started running to lose weight, but actually it's quite— running is quite a good mood lifter. It's your endorphins and things, isn't it? So I probably run every other day. I used to run more… but it was a bit obsessive.'

She says she might feel stressed if she hasn't been for a run, and that exercise can be as addictive as alcohol, although she thinks – as addictions go – it's probably a healthy one.

'I have done 10Ks; I wouldn't run a marathon.'

The training regimen for a marathon is indeed intense.

Emily agrees: 'It's really sore! Chaffing and…! I did the Three Peaks – three mountains in twenty-four hours. Which was good fun, but if I did that again, I'd spend more time. It was a really beautiful thing to do, but I did it in such a rush, I didn't actually get all of the views, so it would've been nice – if I did that again, I would've done a day a mountain.'

This is one of the ironies of modern adulthood – we are constantly rushing around, trying to achieve goals – run 10K, a marathon, climb three mountains in twenty-four hours. So many people I have met have done these things, but as Emily said, did they have time to look around and see the world they were rushing past?

I am often disappointed by things you are 'supposed to do'. Being herded like a sheep through the Sistine Chapel in Rome was one of the most unrewarding experiences of my life. I would prefer to look at the images in a book, quietly in my sitting room, without all the people. Churches and beautiful mountains ought to feel still and contemplative, and tourism at speed often ruins that.

I ask Emily next about how she feels about recent political events. We are still reeling from 2016 – Brexit, the election of Trump in America – after all.

'I think it's worrying that there's such a right-wing shift, and I don't understand how that's happened, or how people can be so self-interested, given how developed we are in lots of other areas. Our technology is developing – seems to be well above our capability to empathize or live with each other. I find it really weird. I mean, Brexit bothers me, but it doesn't bother me as much as I suppose Trump does. What I think is worrying is that our children are not taught politics from a young age, so I think there's lots of people that don't understand about left wing and right wing, which will probably be strange to you because your parents probably talked about it. Certainly, in my class, it's like no one was taught that, and I think there's a big difference. People have entangled the issue of immigration with their politics, so even though they might have three kids and need tax credits, they will vote Conservative, which will take all that away, because they don't want immigration to come in. Because no one's explained to them, "Look, if you vote for UKIP because you don't want people to come in, they'll remove your child benefits. You don't understand – it's a right-wing party!"'

Emily can say this because she still has roots in the area where we grew up and hesitates between identifying as working class and middle class. She is observing it from the ground. Emily thinks the tabloid press feed information to people with a limited education, who then lack the critical faculties to act in their own self-interest.

'There should be, as a society, more obligation – we should be teaching our children, "You can believe what you want, but this is how politics works. This is right wing, this is left wing, this is what socialism is, this is what communism is." I don't think people know that! And because people don't know that, we're in a situation where people are voting without any real knowledge... so they're voting on feelings.'

I wonder if any of us are really informed. Don't we all vote on feelings, to an extent?

I ask Emily about the specific pressures on women who live in her area. Although there are pockets of deprivation here, overall it is a wealthy place – gym membership and personal trainers are the norm. Emily thinks this does impact on her and her daughter.

'Yes, there is an expectation about how you look, and there's a judgement, but actually more from other women bizarrely. So those women at the school gates that are having Botox and running every day to keep fit, I think are quite judgemental if other women aren't doing that. Some of those women are like Stepford Wives!' (Younger readers will not remember this, but *The Stepford Wives* was a 1975 film in which the seemingly perfect housewives in a Connecticut suburb turn out to be robots controlled by their husbands... some have interpreted it as a feminist manifesto exposing the patriarchy.)[70]

But Emily does worry about how she looks, and says, 'I have to be careful not to put that on my daughter. Even though I know it's wrong, we still don't want to be fat, we still don't want to be a size sixteen, we still want to look attractive.'

We talk about how, in your forties, it's the time you need to really accept ageing – otherwise it's a futile attempt to fight it.

Emily says, 'I read an interesting thing that said – it was an older woman talking to a younger woman – and she was saying, "Oh, I just need to get my face done..." and the older woman was like, "No one's told you, have they? That actually it's just – you don't get any younger. You can keep doing this to yourself, but it's inevitable – you are going to be ageing. And at some point, you've got to accept it!"'

We talk lastly about what's changed since we were young, and the conversation comes around to social media. I say that social media has, in some ways, unexpectedly made it much more difficult to connect with people on a real, human level. People tend to 'curate' and offer the official version of their lives on Facebook and Instagram, etc., and they don't want to go beneath that.

Emily says, 'Yeah. You can be quite detached from yourself. You can protect yourself, can't you? So, with social media, you can protect your image, and safeguard your image in a way that gives you a lot of... I suppose security. I quite like social media. I'm on it way too much if I'm honest, oversharing! But I think you're right – you can edit your life, and I do think it makes people a bit detached. I am guilty sometimes, if I don't want to speak to someone, of just texting them, because I don't want to have a conversation!'

We end up talking about our children and social media. Personally, I am dreading the day my now ten-year-old daughter connects to that world. Now feels like an era of innocence and freedom from all those pressures, and I don't want it to end. But at some point, it will, because this is how young people connect today. We used to phone, write letters, and just hang out in the same place, reading and chatting about TV and magazines. Now, the information youngsters need passes through social-media networks. Emily has another theory about this.

'I think they're not gonna use it. Olivia is completely disinterested. She's not worried whether she's got friends or not. She's quite confident. I think we're doing it because it's a massive generational thing, but I suspect when they get older, they'll be like, "Yeah, my parents did that, I can't be bothered with that, I'm not putting that I had a coffee on Facebook!" I think it's gonna be like something that happened... a phase.'

Emily says that advances in artificial intelligence might be worrying, if only because we may not be able humanly to keep up with it.

'Technology is advancing so fast that we haven't got the... like, emotionally, we haven't grown, humanly we haven't advanced enough to deal with the technology. It's about to take out a lot of service jobs… and they're saying, which will never happen, there needs to be some sort of… universal credit, because in forty years, we won't need to have waitresses.'

This idea of a universal basic income is starting to gain traction in some countries. But Emily, clearly influenced by the views of the affluent people she sees around her, is not convinced.

'Sadly, there's too many rich people that won't let that happen!'

5

Emma

During her secondary-school years, Emma lived in the estate next door to our school. Until the age of ten she lived with her mother, father, and sister – a conventional nuclear family – and attended primary school in a nearby village. For reasons that become evident during the conversation, Emma moved away from her home town in her twenties and now lives on the coast in the South West of England. She is a year past forty and completed her training as a nurse twelve years ago. A single parent, Emma has a sixteen-year-old daughter, Milly, and today she works as a specialist nurse in one of the country's leading neonatal units. She is planning to go back to university this year to qualify as a nurse practitioner. These are highly skilled nurses with advanced training allowing them to carry out complex medical procedures and prescribe medicines.

'Once I've qualified, then I'll be a nurse practitioner… that's what I've always wanted to do. When I went into nursing that was where I wanted to end up, so I feel like it's taken longer than I anticipated. But it's quite a nice feeling to finally be on the way to doing what I went into nursing for. Hopefully financially, for Milly and everything, in terms of all the things she's going to need – weddings, cars, houses, and things – then that will sort me out so that I can afford those kinds of things.'

Emma's road to financial security, career, and family success has been long and difficult. Everything she has achieved she has done alone, with no support from her wider family, from whom she is largely estranged.

Emma's daughter, who has just achieved a string of brilliant GCSE grades, is about to take her Grade 8 singing exam, and is leaving home soon to study performing arts at college. She is intelligent, accomplished, and driven – a product of the secure and loving upbringing that Emma has given her. A far cry, therefore, from the 'ill-raised, ignorant, aggressive, and illegitimate' progeny of the much-maligned working-class single mothers stigmatized by former Prime Minister Boris Johnson, in comments written in 1995, soon after we finished school.[71]

Emma's successes and her ebullient and optimistic attitude ('Don't worry,' she tells me, 'I'm quite an open book!') are all the more surprising for the facts of her childhood, which was marked first and foremost with grief after the sudden death of her mother when Emma was still in primary school.

'So my mum died when I was ten, when I was in middle school, and then my dad remarried eighteen months later, which caused a massive rift in my family.'

Emma's maternal grandparents and aunt refused to speak to her father after his marriage. It is common for men to remarry soon after a bereavement, within a year or two, and Emma describes the loss of her mother as sudden and traumatic but only vaguely remembered.

'I think she had an aneurism. She was ill for a couple of weeks… I can remember her dropping us off at school and having to pull over a couple of times because she felt really sick and headachy. She basically just collapsed at work. She was a dinner lady at my sister's school, which I feel was probably really traumatic for my sister, and my sister doesn't remember much about it.

'I can remember my dad coming into my classroom in the middle of the day and saying to the teacher, "We need to take her out," and I don't remember much else, to be honest, apart from the fact that there was a school fête on the Saturday.'

Emma's mother was dying in hospital, but it is the everyday concerns that intrude and distract when there are no words or frame of reference with which to talk about matters of life and death.

'I didn't really understand much about what was happening… and then there was the school fête on the Saturday that I really wanted to go to, and we weren't allowed to go. When I look back now, I think, *Oh my God, that's so awful,* but I just don't think I had any concept of how serious it was.'

Emma didn't see her mother before she died.

'My dad wouldn't let me go and see her. We wanted to go and visit her in hospital, and he said, "No, because your mum always wanted to look her best, and she wouldn't want you to see her looking not her best."'

There was no recognition of what was happening and no goodbye. Emma's father was undoubtedly trying to protect his daughters from what he was feeling as he watched his family fall apart. Emma's mother died that weekend, and her death was handled in a way typical of the era – by never talking about it, and by continuing as though nothing had happened. Our parents were the children of a generation which had suffered unspeakable loss through war, and who had learnt to remain buttoned up, to not speak, to soldier on. It was a collective grief that, as Emma would go on to tell me, her father could not cope with, instead opting to replace their mother quickly with a stepmother, the wound of loss being patched over but never allowed to heal.

Emma says, 'It finished my relationship with my dad, to be honest, because I think I never got over the fact that he wouldn't let us go and see her, so for me, none of it was real. I went to school one day, she dropped me off, and I just never saw her again. I know now, as a nurse, when we let our parents see horrible things that have happened to their babies, and you want to shield them from it… and the doctors say to you, "No, you have to," because they have to understand what's gone wrong.'

Emma's father was ill equipped emotionally to help his daughters, and her story shows starkly how grief suppressed can rip the heart out of a family.

'He can't deal with any of that stuff. Over the years, he basically just buried it. He never, ever spoke about her. I can remember in the early weeks, getting out a photo album to go through and just delving into it, looking at all these pictures, and he came in and he slammed it shut, and he was like, "Well, you're just upsetting yourself, aren't you?" And so I learnt very young to hide all my emotions, especially from him, and that was it. I don't have any solid memories of what she was like as a person or what she was like as a mum, because he never spoke about her – he never kept that memory alive.'

Emma tells me that her father's silence, and his decision to remarry, eventually destroyed their relationship. He must have believed that, in remarrying, he was giving his two young daughters a new mother. By ignoring their loss, he perhaps felt he was protecting them from the intolerable pain of loss. But Emma believes these two events combined to make her later childhood profoundly unhappy. She no longer sees or speaks to her father, after years of trying to repair the damage done, and trying to create a grandparent relationship with her daughter. She is now beyond any feelings of bitterness.

'Just to be able to cut him out is such a relief, to be honest… That family bond was broken so many years ago now.'

Having her daughter, Milly, on her own was a challenge, without the support of immediate or extended family.

'When she was first born, I remember it really brought everything back. There are always significant moments in your life, aren't there, where you miss family members or whatever? I was incredibly vulnerable, and I think that was probably the first time I actually had some counselling.'

Emma says that she lacked any 'frame of reference to mother a child'. When she asked her dad for advice on the early years and looking after a baby, he couldn't help – '"Oh, I can't remember – your mum did all that."'

Emma's counsellor suggested that she might have chosen to become a children's nurse in order to learn how to mother. This makes sense to Emma, who says that she had a practical idea of how to care for a child and keep it healthy but lacked any memories of playing with her mother.

'I wouldn't say I'm a natural mother. I never found doing the fun stuff, like throwing glitter everywhere and arts and crafts and that stuff, very easy.

'Growing up, I had my stepmum, who I didn't get on with, two stepbrothers who... we mutually hated each other really, and a stepsister who was... I don't know how to describe her! She was a bit of a punk and into alcohol... she used to come round and get really drunk and break things, and eventually, my dad barred her from the house, because she hit me one day.

'So that ruined my life really... in terms of my childhood, because I just hated being at home; I hated the environment. It was always my stepmum and her family versus me and my sister and my dad, although my dad was so weak that he never really stuck up for us.'

The conflict that Emma describes in her home is entirely in line with what research has shown about the difficulty of integrating step-parents into the home, especially where there has been a bereavement. It is sometimes called the 'Cinderella effect', whereby a child is much more likely to be ill treated by a step-parent than by a biological parent. In our generation, as divorce rates ran high, stepfamily conflicts were very common.[72]

Secondary school for Emma came only a couple of years after losing her mother. She remembers feeling 'absolutely petrified' of going up to our school.

'I remember the stories about how you all had to shower together, and how they would check your towels to see if they were wet to make sure you'd been in. I think probably in our second or third year at Highfield, they got cubicles, didn't they?'

We were certainly relieved to be given that little bit of privacy, to be spared the indignity of sharing a shower room with five other naked girls.

At school, Emma says she was part of a 'middle layer' of pupils, 'essentially quite bright, not overly clever and geeky'. She was mature, in a way.

'I had to grow up quickly because I brought myself up from the age of twelve or whatever.'

She managed to keep on an even keel at school. Despite her anger, and the violence and chaos at home, which led to her bunking off school in fifth form, there was something keeping her engaged. She was frustrated at sixteen to still be treated like a child, despite her 'normal' childhood having effectively ended at the age of ten.

'I desperately wanted to leave home. My home life was just abysmal... I just hated every minute I had to be at home.' This seems to have driven her educational focus just long enough to get her over the hurdle of GCSEs.

'I wanted to just throw it all to the wall and be like, "Well I actually don't care." But I had this inner sense that was saying to me, "You do need to get your GCSEs – this will make a difference to your future, you know, knuckle down." So I did for a while do stupid things, and we bunked off and did things that we shouldn't have done, but at the end of it, I probably still went home and did my homework and made sure that it got handed in on time. And I think that's the kind of person Milly is now, and the person that I was and still am.'

Emma's determination, I suggest, is rooted in an underlying sense of self-belief and dignity.

'I remember clearly struggling to get through my exams, because nobody was making me do it. They weren't even facilitating it ... so I don't know quite how I made myself do it, to be honest. I think it was just my own – probably the same as Milly – for my own pride, and my own self-esteem, to say, "Actually, I will do it."'

This stubbornness has been crucial to Emma in providing a safe, financially secure and loving home life for her daughter. She found in herself the capacity to keep going when it would have been easier to give up.

When Emma hit the wall emotionally and intellectually during her nursing training, she again turned to her father for help, and again he failed her.

'I got halfway through the second year. I was struggling financially... Milly was five, it was tricky juggling everything, and I phoned him, and I said, "I really think I'm gonna quit... I need to work full-time, I'm skint, the work's really hard, blah blah blah," and he said to me, "Well, don't worry, because if you give up now, you've done better than any of us ever thought you could anyway."'

The insult of her father's low expectations, reasons Emma, impelled her to complete her training.

'It was the drive I needed. I went out, and I found another part-time job – I think I cleaned in a bank or something – and I finished that course just to spite him! Because I thought, *How dare you? how dare you tell me I can't do it?* And I think through my life, really, that has been my motivation. Tell me that I can't do something, and I'll do it twice as well.'

Emma had left school as soon as she could, at sixteen.

'I went straight to work in Tesco, literally from the day I left school.'

Emma made new friends at work, left home, and moved in with one of them while she saved up a deposit to buy a house. In terms of young working people being able to think about buying their own house, this was a different era: for young people in low-paid jobs today, it seems an impossible dream.

Emma's first boyfriend had lived a few doors down from her.

'I look back now, and I'm horrified, because I was fourteen and he was twenty-one, and he was literally the boy next door. He still lived at home with his parents, he had a motorbike, he used to come and pick me up from school on his motorbike, and I went out with him for four years and thought he was amazing. I used to stay round his house, and my dad, every now and again, would just say to me, "Oh, when you stay there, you do stay in the spare room, don't you?" And I'd be like, "Yeah, yeah," and that was the extent of it – and I didn't obviously.'

This first boyfriend was passive and impressionable.

'The first time we had sex was when I was sixteen and that was instigated by me, so I did wait until it was legal or whatever, but as soon as I got to twenty-one, I looked back and thought, *Who dates a fourteen-year-old?*'

After leaving home, it was a time of freedom and experimentation for Emma.

'And then boyfriends – oh, shocking, really, when I look back now! Just one every couple of weeks, which is hideous, and now… I think, *Oh God, what a tramp!* But I think I was desperately lonely, and was probably just replacing what I wasn't getting at home by having lots of boyfriends, which was all very fun at the time, and it's all quite harmless, you know?'

Harmless or not, relationships with men have been complicated for Emma. Although men clearly find her attractive, long-term relationships have been difficult to sustain. She says that she wants to control things, which, she reflects, is a reaction to the uncontrollably traumatic events of her childhood.

'Over the years, so there's a couple of long relationships I've had. I've always got on with their mums really well.'

Emma feels that she put up with relationships that were not working because she liked being part of another person's family.

'The thing that I've missed is the relationship that I had with their family.'

Emma was mature and decisive in the areas of her life that really mattered, given how little obvious guidance was there. I wonder if her strong sense of self-worth and motivation came from her mother, whether through inherited temperament or nurture; Emma managed to look after herself in teenage sexual relationships and to finish her GCSEs and get good marks.

She thinks she agrees: 'Now, I'm finding it really difficult with my daughter, because I can't control everything anymore, because she's sixteen, and she needs to do her own thing. It's hard for me to let her make her own mistakes and try not to control everything. One of the reasons I think my daughter's so similar to me is because I've brought her up with those same values. I must have got them from somewhere, and actually I'd never thought of it like that. Obviously there are probably parts of me that are closely determined by how she brought me up, even though I can't remember them.'

One long-term relationship during Emma's early twenties lasted four years. She worked at Tesco's for a decade, so she was able to transfer to different branches in order to move area – she moved all over the South of England during this time – always intending to 'look for something else'. The man Emma lived with was divorced, and she says the relationship worked because, 'I wanted to get away from my family, he wanted to get away from his ex-wife, so we moved to the South West.

'I spent four years with him. He had a vasectomy after he'd had his two children; he was thirty-three and he didn't want any more kids, so that was really, really hard, because I did, I wanted children. And we talked about him having that reversed, and he said yes, and then he would change his mind a few weeks later. I realize now he was a complete alcoholic, and he would go out on a Saturday night and not come home till Monday morning, and sometimes I'd have his children during that time! So he was an okay bloke, but he had a lot of problems, and then we split up.'

Emma decided it was also time to move on jobwise.

'Again, I transferred with Tesco, except this time, I think I did two days and realized that I absolutely hated it and left. So for the first time ever, I didn't have a job, and then I got a job on a milk round. I think I did it for about eighteen months and really loved it.'

Emma bought out her ex-boyfriend's share in the house they co-owned and took in friends as lodgers.

'There was a girl that came to work on the milk round as well, so she moved in, because it was a four-bedroom house – really not a very nice four-bedroom house! – but she moved in, and then it became a bit of a refuge! There was a girl, a friend of mine, who'd split up with her boyfriend and was pregnant – she moved in. And then we all went on a holiday to Turkey... which resulted in one of the girls leaving her fiancé, and when she did finally come back to the country, her parents kicked her out, so she came and lived with me!'

Emma met the father of her daughter, who was Turkish, on another holiday.

'I met Milly's dad... I'd just got out of a long-term relation-ship, and I think he was telling me all the things I wanted to hear, and it was just a total escape. My friends were paying me enough money that I was covering my mortgage, and I was in and out of work with the milk round – that was all quite casual work – and then I would just skip off to Turkey for a couple of weeks here and there. And eventually I left the milk round, and I went out there to live for six months. So I'd lived with him and his family – they lived right on the border with Syria.'

Emma's holiday romance went further than she expected.

'When I came back, I realized I was pregnant. I couldn't get back into my job… they weren't employing anybody.'

Emma now found herself in a precarious situation – pregnant, jobless, and without further education qualifications.

'It was a chaotic time in my life, and it was really tricky. I didn't tell any of my family until I was five months pregnant, because I didn't know what the hell I was going to do – I was essentially out of work, I was only just covering the mortgage by the rent my friends were paying me, because they were literally paying me just scraps here and there, I never really had any formal agreements with them, so I was getting more and more into debt, more and more behind with my mortgage, and basically didn't have a job… I'd never been on benefits in my life, and stupidly, I thought that the longer I tried to be self-sufficient and didn't claim, that it would go in my favour.'

It would have been better for her to claim housing benefit earlier, but she had no way of knowing this.

'I had absolutely no concept of the benefit system. I'd never had to use it, I'd worked from the day I left school, so got myself into a bit of a pickle really.'

Emma ended up having to sell her house to settle her debts. She returned to Turkey for a month, coming back when she was seven months pregnant, then moved to another town on the south coast to be near a friend.

'So I rented a very small flat in town, paid my six months' rent upfront, had to go and sign on every week, standing in the queue seven months pregnant. You have to prove you're looking for work, so I would rock up to all these interviews, heavily pregnant, hidden under a coat, but you know, not very well hidden. And obviously I never got any of the jobs. I had to do that for a month. It was the most humiliating and degrading time of my life.'

Yet, ironically, Emma discovered that in terms of gaining new skills and qualifications, she was in a better position being on benefits than earning.

'I was entitled to a lot more free educational things, so I could go to college and didn't have to pay for it. I went back to college, got a little part-time job in a nursing home to give me some experience of care, because I'd never worked in care before. And then when Milly was three, I went to uni and did my nurse training. I think I was twenty-eight when I started, and my nan was like, "For God's sake, why didn't you do it when you left school? … Now you're trying to do it with a three-year-old!"'

Emma fitted her work around her young daughter's routine.

'The benefit was that when she went to bed at seven, eight o'clock at night, she stayed in bed, so I did all my studying in the evening. As opposed to now, when I'm getting phone calls like "Can you come and pick me up from here?" I can't get a damn thing done!

'I did my nurse training and here I am now! And actually I'd forgotten… in the process of all that, I did go bankrupt as well. I was in so much debt from my house… I just didn't know what to do. I had no advice. I think I might have gone to Citizens' Advice a couple of times, but it always felt like they were elderly people that were working there voluntarily. And if you asked them a question, they would get out a Yellow Pages or something, and I thought, *Christ, I can do that myself!*'

Having her young daughter was the impetus Emma needed to make some decisions about her future.

'I thought, *I really need to get my act together here.* I needed to put down some roots, and that was what drove me to get it all sorted. I went bankrupt so that I could clear all of the debt. Which obviously screwed my financial life for the next six years.'

Emma couldn't get any kind of loan after that, but she says it was a relief to be free of temptation. She didn't want any more debt and knew how easy it would be to lose everything.

'I worked so many jobs, I worked so hard to buy my first house, which is fine, but then something unexpected happens, like getting pregnant and losing your job at the same time – it's gone in a flash.'

That Emma lost her way financially perhaps reflects the early trauma of losing her mother and the lack of guidance she had from then on.

'I felt like I made a lot of really, really shit decisions because I didn't have anybody to talk to about them.'

Emma returned to college to complete an Access course on Health and Social Care, which led to a diploma in children's nursing. This was made possible by a non-means-tested bursary. Soon afterwards, the system changed to a means-tested bursary for a degree programme, which Emma says she would not have been able to afford.

Emma realized the relationship with Milly's father was the definition of a holiday romance – something that works on holiday and not when you get home.

'I think when I was in Turkey, I was completely charmed by him. And when I came back to the UK, I realized that, actually, they tell you what you want to hear. He only ever wanted to enter this country. He was desperate for us to get married so that he could come and live here… Every time I went to Turkey, I would say to my friends, "Do not let me take all the paperwork that you need to get married!" I knew it wasn't the right thing.'

When Emma found out she was pregnant, she still had every intention of making a life with him somehow.

'After she was born, he was actually trying to come over at that time. He was trying all these illegal routes and people smuggling, essentially, to try and get over to the UK, and couldn't. So I bought a ticket to take her out to Turkey when she was about… six weeks old? … and then 9/11 happened, and I thought, *I can't do it*. I remember sitting watching it on the telly, thinking, *I can't put her on a plane; I can't fly out to a Muslim country*. I was absolutely terrified. I just cancelled it, and that was it really. The longer I didn't go, the more frightened of him I became, and thought, *God, what if he is really angry with me and he takes her off me?*'

At times Emma has regretted that her daughter never knew her father while growing up, but her fear of losing Milly prevented her from establishing meaningful contact.

'I always told her about him, so as she grew up, she would cry in her bed, and say, "I want to know my daddy." And I'd be like, "Oh, God," but then I'd just put the news on, and I'd see a woman sat in an airport in Dubai… Islamic law always favours the dad, and I'd see that in front of my face, and I'd think, *I can't do it, because what if I take her out there and he snatches her and I never see her?'*

For Emma this emotional tug-of-war continued until her daughter's father managed to locate her on Facebook when she was sixteen.

This has led to some contact being established. Milly's father managed to get to the UK in the end and has married a woman in Scotland.

'He messaged Milly, and that was it. They met and they see each other – infrequently though. She's not that bothered unfortunately.'

He even contacted Emma to say that he wanted to leave his wife and come and live with her, but by this stage, she was wise to the nature of the relationship, to its fantasies and realities.

'I'm quite happy on my own; this is how it should be, and I don't think we were ever really meant to be. I think we filled a gap for each other at the time, but it never felt like something that was sustainable, because we were so different. He was a very strict Muslim, and I'm not even the kind of person that would put a meal on the table for a guy five days a week! For a holiday it was great, but in real life, I just don't think it ever would have worked. I'm just not subservient woman material really!'

Emma connects with the common sentiment that turning forty opens up a stage of life where we begin to appreciate our own mortality, our parents' decline, and we need to learn how to mellow and forgive – a feeling also expressed by other interviewees. I ask her if she feels that her anger towards her father has abated in recent years. Emma pauses.

'That anger is what drove me for a long time. It kind of had its benefits because it stopped me getting upset. The thing that stopped me crying about it, like I did when I was a child, was the fact that I could just be like, "Well, he's a horrible person." When I had my daughter, I became even more angry, because I thought, *How could you have done this to me? I'd never do that to her!*'

Having Milly flicked an emotional switch in Emma, one which had been turned off since her mother's death.

'All of a sudden, I had somebody to relate it to who I would never treat that way, so it made the way he treated me, or even neglected me emotionally, I think, even worse.' Even the arrival of his grandchild was not enough to heal old wounds.

'I had some counselling and I spoke to him and told him the things that I needed from him, and he couldn't... They said, "Get him to write you a letter. If he can't talk to you, get him to write some things down." And he couldn't even do that, and over time I just began to care a little bit less and a little bit less.'

In her description of this inadequate father, Emma hints at a remaining kernel of connection. She no longer feels anything, good or bad, for him, but she wants her daughter to be able to see him if she wants to.

'I said to Milly, "If you want to see him, I will take you up there, I'll meet halfway, I'll do all these things." But she didn't. He wrote to her once a year, Christmas and birthdays, and writes in the cards, "Come and visit if you want; I'll come and pick you up." She doesn't bother.'

So the man who could not put pen to paper to tell his daughter what she meant to him, to tell her about the numbing grief that cast a shadow over her childhood and adolescence, could nonetheless be relied upon to offer a lift. I wonder if this is a common marker of our parents' generation. My own father, who'd been sent to boarding school at seven, always had delayed emotional reactions. But he was always available to offer a lift. He would drive us hundreds of miles if we asked, but only in much later life could he say, 'I love you.'

Emma says, 'I really tried, as she was growing up, to take her up there and to facilitate for them to have a relationship. But I'm not sad about it anymore. I'm not angry about it anymore. But it's funny, isn't it, how it takes you that long?'

By forty, we cease to be young, and many of us start to realize the extent to which anger saps the life from us.

Emma agrees: 'Yeah! You just don't have the energy for it. Especially when you have kids... you have so many other things to put your energy into, and that is a massive drain on your emotional life.'

She thinks life is very different for young girls growing up today, compared to the 1980s and '90s when we came of age.

'I don't know whether it's the internet, or the peer pressure... I feel like when we were at school, yes, there were people that were bullied, and there were friendship groups that fell out. But I don't ever remember it being really debilitating and taking over people's lives. I feel like the pressure that Milly had at school, not just the relationships that she had with her teachers that weren't particularly good, but between her so-called friends, was absolutely horrendous. So much pressure for the things that they wear, for the way they behave, the way they speak, the phone they've got. And Milly's quite sensitive, and although she can be quite sharp and very headstrong herself, ultimately, if someone was crying in the corner, she would be the one that would go over and ask them what was wrong.'

Another change, though, is that awareness of mental-health issues has increased, and so has the support available. Emma's daughter is one of many children today accessing these resources. Emma thinks it's because bullying is a more serious problem now.

'I just don't remember kids being that nasty when we were growing up... I don't remember it being that stressful. For the last couple of years at school, Milly saw one woman who was a support worker, and there was someone else that I think was a psychologist, and she went and spent time in the office with them, just to talk about all of that stuff. And my reaction at first was, *There was none of this when we were at school; the kids these days, they just need to man up.* And then I thought, *Actually, no, we didn't have anything like the pressure they face.*'

Emma says girls seem to grow up more quickly now and are sexualized younger than in our generation. I reply that in some respects the world today seems more gendered than it was in the 1980s, when often girls and boys wore the same clothes and had the same short haircuts.

'You're right, it has. A bit vain, isn't it? This self-obsession with selfies and Snapchat and like, my God, what is that teaching people? That it's not okay to look normal anymore?'

We did of course worry, too, about hair and make-up – Emma remembers, for example, her father's main punishment being to ban her from wearing make-up to school. But although we could look in the mirror in the morning and worry about our faces, spots, and make-up, there was no incessant reflecting back of a girl's image via selfies and social media.

It's interesting to listen to a woman reflecting on her experiences as a teen while managing her own daughter's journey. Emma is always immaculately presented – not a hair out of place, make-up done, snappily dressed. Perhaps like her mother, who'd 'always looked her best'. But Emma's daughter has a different style.

'I'm really chuffed because my daughter's style is quite sort of grungy… She wears a lot of baggy trousers and big oversized tops and doesn't brush her hair for a week. She's not plastered in foundation with fake eyelashes and fake nails, and a lot of her friends, they all did the red lipstick thing – Milly tried it and she was like, "Oh my God, I look ridiculous," and I was like, "Yeah, you do, take it off!" … Very quickly, she decided for herself that, "Actually, Mum, do you know what, I think I look better without make-up on anyway."'

Emma is upbeat about the future, and is now preparing to return to university to complete her nurse-practitioner training, as previously mentioned.

'I'm quite chuffed, although I'm nervous about going back to uni and doing it all again for a year, financially, this is where I needed to be. I just want to be able to give Milly a little bit of a start as she grows up, so if I can afford to buy her a first car… get her on the housing ladder maybe… and essentially pay for her wedding, then I will at least feel like I've given her the stepping stone, and I think she'll do the rest. She's a much happier person since she's left school.'

It's interesting to me that Emma, who has never married or seen marriage as a necessary marker of maturity, envisages these conventional steps towards adulthood for her daughter. But this is perhaps because Emma has assumed the role of father and mother to Milly, and she has had to make up both roles as she has gone along.

Despite such a good outcome for Emma as a mother, and educationally for her daughter, Emma still feels guilt about parenting and working. Milly now has an older boyfriend, and Emma does not always get along with him.

'I worry I haven't always done the best thing by her. Obviously by being out at work, I worry that if she's fiercely independent and with this guy because she is lonely like I was, because I was quite absent during her growing up … so I do look back with a little bit of regret, which I knew I would. I knew at the time I was gonna look back and think, *Where did my baby go?*'

Emma looks only to the future now.

'I've bought my first house after all of that bankruptcy and everything. Bought my first house four years ago. When Milly moves out or when she learns to drive, whichever way it works out, I will only ever downsize to a little country cottage and buy some chickens or something! So I feel like, after this year, if I pass this course, and I get into this job, which I think I will love – it's what I've always wanted to do – then I can really, hopefully, start to sit back and think, *Okay!* We've kind of made it, you know? She'll be seventeen, coming on eighteen then, and yeah, hopefully, hopefully…'

6

Alex

Alex and her twin sister Laura grew up in a small town a few miles away from our secondary school, in a detached house within the grounds of a large independent boys' school where their father was a teacher. As girls they attended their local village primary school – we used to call them infants, first, and middle school – before going up to secondary school. They became good friends of mine at school, and we have stayed in touch on and off over the years.

Unusually, for our generation, their mother went back to work as a teacher in a local prep school soon after the birth of a younger sister, Alice, in 1982. Today, Alex lives in the countryside and is deputy head of a rural village primary school in the North of England, about fifteen minutes' drive from her sister Laura, who is a university lecturer. She lives alone in a cottage with her dog and cat, and keeps a couple of horses down the road. Laura is a single mother to two adopted girls, Lily and Sophia, now aged nine and five. Alex is closely involved with bringing up Laura's two daughters. I begin here with Alex's story.

'We had, or have, I'm not really sure, one younger sister, who was born in 1982, who sadly had Down's syndrome. And that's as far as really... we know.'

Their baby sister was given up for adoption soon after her birth, and it's one of the first things Alex tells me about. In 1976, when we were born, and indeed in the year Alice was born, there was no routine prenatal screening available for expectant mothers.[73] Every story is different, but this one shows the reality of what sometimes happened in a time when women did not have the choices they have today. The choices people make in these situations are often instinctive, always difficult, and can have far-reaching and unexpected consequences. Neither Alex nor Laura knows very much about why their mother reacted in the way she did, and how she has faced her loss over the years.

We associate Down's syndrome with older mothers, women in their forties at least, but Alex's mother was only in her mid-thirties when she had Alice. There was no reason to expect she was particularly at risk of having a child with a disability. When Alex and Laura were born, their mother hadn't known she was expecting twins until she was in labour. It was commonly very late in pregnancy that two heartbeats (or more) could be detected, so women who had multiple births often didn't know how many babies they were carrying until they arrived. Alex's mother had already had this – admittedly happier – shock to contend with, so a second pregnancy resulting in an unexpected discovery was extremely difficult – beyond, I think, what we can imagine.

In our conversation, I try to make the connection between these two birth experiences with Alex, and she acknowledges it was 'another difficult shock... really sad... something she didn't know'. Before they started their own families, Laura and Alex had tentatively begun the process of finding their sister, but as Alex puts it, 'We hit a massive brick wall.' They had not wanted to involve their parents, and the mixed feelings are still there. Even when one decides not to pursue a lost relative, or a family secret, these things often remain unfinished business.

'Funnily enough, Laura mentioned it again fairly recently, of "Should we?" and my feeling is, no, I don't think we should do any more to trace Alice. Because I don't know what one would do, if you do find that person. It's really hard.'

Alex seems a little conflicted here, as though hesitating between a residual feeling of connection to this sister she never knew, and a deep loyalty to and wish to protect her parents, whose experience this primarily was. But Alice has always been named, which was one way of saying that, although they could not keep her, they recognized her humanity and her existence. Alex and Laura have always, in the whole time I have known them, spoken openly about what happened.

Alex's recollections of primary school are vague.

'Do you know, it's weird, I can remember so little... I remember thinking I was pretty thick at school. Because I couldn't spell, and I couldn't remember my times tables. Obviously it transpired that I was dyslexic, which was why I couldn't spell or remember my times tables!'

Alex muddled through primary school, a period marked by the loss of her younger sister, and I wonder if this lack of memory reflects the difficult time the family went through. When she arrived at secondary school in September 1988, she remembers 'being faintly surprised that I was in top sets for things... I'd think, *I thought I was really stupid!*'

Alex and Laura's parents had planned to send them on a teachers' bursary to a boarding school near the south coast, but, in the end, they didn't have the heart to send them away. Once again, I wonder if, having handed over one child to the care of someone else, it was too difficult to do so again, even though their twin daughters were eleven years old.

Alex doesn't quite make this connection, but she does refer to her father's attachment to his daughters.

'I think when push came to shove, I think the old bloke, particularly, didn't want us going off to boarding school, which I think is good, because I don't think we'd have enjoyed that either... because he's an old softie! And he would have missed us, quite simply. Which I think is the right thing really.'

Alex's memories of going up to secondary school are similarly vague.

'I remember being very excited about the fact that we were going to do lots of different subjects. I remember I was really pissed off that they put Laura and me in completely different houses so we never saw each other, because that was their weird sort of twin policy.'

Schools often deliberately separate twins, and some parents also favour this, but Alex strongly feels that such policies are wrongheaded, and that twins should be allowed to decide for themselves.

'In my school, in my capacity as deputy head, my experience is that every set of twins, and we have three, are in different classes. I think it's absolutely fine if the parents and teachers have asked the twins, and that's what they want. But I don't suppose for one minute they have. It's something that I need to get my head round a bit more… just to make sure that actually, that is what they want.'

I ask Alex to talk about her experience of being a twin. Her first response is obvious, that of course she and Laura have never known anything different.

'I think it's something I really like… and I think it is why we're so close, and yet, Kelly and Dawn [another pair of twin girls in our year at school] weren't so close, were they? But I also think that we were quite fortunate in that we were not dressed the same.'

In our year at school, which had around 200 pupils, there were five sets of twins, three sets of same-sex 'identical' twins, and two sets of boy-girl twins. The fraternal twins were more or less like normal siblings that happened to be in the same year group, but there was a much more obvious symbiosis and closeness in the cases of the identical twins.

Alex feels that their parents did not lay too much emphasis on their twin-ness: 'We were just two children, rather than… you know, "the twins".'

I suggest that their parents must have seen them as quite different people, and Alex agrees. Yet partly because of their closeness as children, and partly because of where they lived, geographically, in relation to our school, Alex doesn't feel that she made many lasting friendships at school. Her close friendships have come later in life. Alex says she read recently that a person can only really have six close friends, which she says is, 'good… and incredibly normal', in contrast to the world of social-media 'friends' which 'is actually complete bollocks'.

Alex is academically able and conscientious, so she did very well at school, despite her dyslexia. But for sixth form, she and Laura decided to leave our state secondary school to go to the boys' private school where their father was a teacher, and which was just about to admit girls into the sixth form.

'I really didn't want to stay at Highfield. It just never felt like a very warm sort of school, I think. It always felt a bit like you were just a number.'

This was a feeling many of us had – of just being a face in a crowd, in marked contrast to the privilege of the girls' grammar school education many of our mothers had enjoyed. As Mary Ingham recalled when she went to her high school, 'I gazed at the names inscribed in gold in the entrance hall, when we all went separately with our mothers for the introductory interview with the headmistress before the term began.'[74]

At our school, there were no gilded names and not a single one-to-one conversation with the teachers. At my children's secondary school today, each new pupil has an introductory meeting with the headteacher and I think it does lay the groundwork for loyalty to the school. It is a way of welcoming a child into the school community and making them feel valued.

Alex also says that our comprehensive did not offer the same academic opportunities as the private school, especially in subjects like English and Art. The private schooling the girls received in sixth form turned out to be a good academic investment, but it was a huge social challenge.

'They promised there were going to be lots of girls in the year, and then in the end, they all dropped out, apart from one other and us. So… socially, it was extremely difficult.'

Alex and Laura were surrounded by a 'bunch of boys that had never known any girls around them before'. They both studied the same A level subjects – English, History, and Art – and both gained straight A grades. Laura won a place at an Oxford college to read English, and Alex went to university at Durham, following what was then (and still is to some extent) the standard trajectory of the most academically able, privately educated children. One reason parents pay school fees is to achieve access to these elite institutions, as well as mastery of 'soft' skills such as self-confidence, engaging conversation, and the networking abilities required for social climbing.

At the boys' private school, Alex had her first experiences with boyfriends.

'I was very close to one boy, who was the head boy. We were good friends all the way through, which was really nice. But I think it was a lot harder to make friends with anybody else. He was just very mature, I think. And I went out with several people there actually.'

I don't remember any of these romances, although I stayed good friends with Alex through sixth form, so she must have been discrete about them.

Alex and Laura landed, aged just sixteen, in a particularly hormonally charged environment. How was this situation, and their evolving sexuality, handled by the school and parents?

Alex says, 'I don't think it was really handled. Just bumbled along!'

This made for awkward moments in the dating experience for Alex.

'I got on well with this guy called Simon, and I invited him round once, and he came into my bedroom, and I remember the old man going absolutely berserk! And me not really getting why, because I had no intention of doing anything other than just chatting with this person and having a nice time. But obviously my parents thought, *Oh my God, there's a boy in her bedroom!*'

Alex took a gap year between school and university, spent a few months travelling in Italy, and worked in a big fashion chain store in a nearby city.

'I started working for Next in my gap year, which obviously turned out to be a really good thing.'

Alex ended up taking on a lot of responsibility at the shop and completed management training, which meant she was able to transfer to a branch in Newcastle, near where she went to university.

University was a difficult time for her, although she continued to excel academically. She became weekend manager of a flagship branch of Next when she was just twenty, whilst during the week she devoted herself to studying. But she says she hated university.

'It was just full of people getting really pissed all the time, and there was no privacy, no home comforts, the accommodation was awful… Again, because I'd worked for most of my gap year, I really hated Durham, and I wanted to leave on many occasions, and my parents were very good at saying, "Oh, just give it another few…"'

Although she stayed and completed her studies, and got a first-class degree, she concludes that the university experience was quite a negative one.

'I didn't go and make the friends that I thought I would. Instead, all I wanted to do was just to go home and have a working life. I just didn't want all this weird socializing, that's all really false, isn't it? And the lack of routine, and… you know, I'm a real homemaker, I think. I really like my space. And it was just awful. And the thing that got me through university was that I had the job at the Next store in Newcastle. And we used to transfer backwards and forwards in the holidays. And I loved the fact that I could a) earn my own money and b) was around normal people who didn't want to get pissed all the time.'

After university Alex decided she wanted to go into teaching, like her parents. They, however, 'just spent their whole time going, "You'll earn no money, and be miserable, and will mark books till eleven o'clock every night." So they really tried to put me off.'

Initially, Alex was dissuaded and worked her way up successfully to the role of area manager in retail, a job she did for several years after graduation. She thinks the delay was a good thing, as she'd originally thought she would teach at a secondary school.

'I looked at senior first, and I went to visit a big comprehensive and it put me off. Just put me off. Because it was like Highfield all over again. It was shabby buildings, massive numbers of kids… kids just pissing around, and massive behaviour management issues.'

But then Alex met someone who was a primary headteacher, who invited her to visit her school.

'And I spent a week in her school, and I loved it, and just knew from that point that I wanted my own class.'

In her manner, tastes and style, Alex presents as quite upper-middle class, but she also seems to have the common touch – she has a gift for dealing with children and young people from all backgrounds.

'I hope so, yeah. I think I'm quite a good communicator.'

At university, surrounded by privileged students whom she superficially resembled – 'green wellies' as she calls them – Alex felt alienated, but she also says, 'When I was at Next, I loved that slightly earthy side of life... which is bizarre, given that I'm also quite a solitary person. But I think I'm very good at falling within a role, where there are rules... that my role requires me to be a certain person and do things a certain way.'

Alex ascribes this to what she terms her ASD – autistic spectrum disorder. This is not a formal diagnosis but something she has gradually come to see in herself and her own personality traits.

'I enjoy my own company. I'm quite particular, and I'm very, very noise sensitive. So that sort of sensory side. I also really don't like physical contact, and it's awful, because Lily [Alex's eight-year-old niece] has this thing about kissing. And I just can't stand it, and you feel so terrible, don't you? Because they want to kiss and cuddle you, because they're little and they love you. And I've always been a bit like that, even with people that I've gone out with, I've not really wanted... I've always had to force myself actually.'

Alex reminds me of one relationship she had with a slightly older man in Durham when she was living and studying there.

'I hated the fact that he... and I think I find this, completely, with men. I've always got to a certain point and then gone, "Actually, no, I'm not interested in you," because they get really possessive. And sort of territorial, and I absolutely detest that!'

Alex casually slips in that she's also had 'the odd girlfriend', but the important point is that she doesn't fit any kind of conventional category, and she doesn't seek out a label – despite the self-diagnosis of ASD. She is happiest on her own, and in control of the close relationships she has with family and friends. What did she envisage for her life, back when we were young? Did she think along conventional lines, that she would get married and have children?

'No, I never, ever, ever, ever— I've always known I would never get married. Absolutely known I would never get married. We've got all these young teachers at my school who are Mrs this and that. And it turns me cold! The thought of being Mrs something.'

The headteacher at Alex's school recently married for the first time, at fifty-three.

'I think a lot of her getting married was purely to get rid of the "Miss". It's a really interesting thing. I think she felt she had to in some way conform. Whereas I have absolutely no need for that, and I don't care! I'm not fussed.'

Alex and I talk a little more about her life alone, and not wishing, or feeling capable of, sharing her space with another person.

'It's a tricky one, because sometimes I think, *Oh God, you're not capable of loving*, and yet, with your family…'

I say that Alex seems full of love for her family – her parents, friends, sister, and her nieces. She just needs space around her in order to love.

'I just feel a bit guilty. I think, actually, I must be incredibly selfish. I'm probably classically bisexual, I reckon. But I don't think I would want to be with a man at all now.'

I ask Alex about children and suggest that she must have made a decision on it at some point. I wonder how she feels at forty, forty-one, having not had children.

'I could've done. But… I didn't want to be pregnant. I had that feeling of really not wanting that. It's a shame, because I did want to adopt, and that is something I had always wanted to do, and that's what I had seen myself as doing, so that was a dream from a young age really.'

Alex still has some regrets about this, and it's partly the result of a difficult and painful experience she had several years earlier. Alex had gone a long way down the route of adopting a five-year-old girl. She was partly motivated by the fact that older children were in great need of adoption placements, and she wanted to give a home to an older child who might otherwise not find a family. But the initial fostering placement was not a success, and it wasn't possible for the child to stay with Alex – for very sensitive and complex reasons that we don't go into during this conversation. The eventual failure of the placement, and the experience of then having to abandon a child who had already been abandoned once by society, left Alex devastated for a time.

'Now I understand that it is not meant to be. And I think my role, really, is as an aunty to my sister's crazy kids!'

I ask her, though, if she would consider adoption again.

'When I came out of it, I was absolutely convinced that I would do it again. But I think, as time moved away, I realized that I couldn't put myself through that again. And Laura already had Lily, and I just realized that, as a family, we didn't have the resource, the physical resource, to take on another child. And I would still maintain that, unless Laura had a partner, it is essential that I'm there to support her.'

So Alex is involved in raising children and is an important adult figure and official legal guardian to her nieces, Lily and Sophia. She is clearly more than just an aunt.

She says, 'I never, ever stopped to think that they're not, like, totally part of the family. I think adoption also brings with it... I think you spend a lot of time feeling a bit of a failure. You're so conscious that these children need so much, and yet you still get cross with them. Or... they push your buttons like kids do, but because they're not your own, there's always that feeling of, "Oh my God, am I failing them? Do I love them enough?" You can feel guilty about just trying to put basic standards and rules in place sometimes.'

Alex says that one or other of the girls, at a given time, can be quite hard work, but that she still loves them just as much.

'I never, ever want them to feel like they're not the most loved thing, because they are. And equally, you're saying, "Right, you've got to bring it down a notch or two," or, "Stop hitting your sister round the head," and I think maybe with birth children you'd never question that... But I think when the children are adopted, you always feel so conscious of the fine line for them, between never having a family and having a family. So it's hard. I think you end up spoiling them more.'

I say that parents generally are very good at feeling guilty about their parenting. I recall times when my children were little, and were difficult, when I have wanted to reassure Laura that some behaviour is just children being, well, children. When my children have behaved in a particularly savage way, I have had the urge to press pause, to take a picture, and be able to show Laura that this is what a birth child is sometimes like too.

Their approach to parenting the children is quite tribal, as the girls are getting their mothering, or parenting, from two different people who are not a couple but part of the same family, and they are supported by a network of friends and extended family – some of whom have also adopted. The setup is unconventional, but it works for them, and for the girls.

I want to ask Alex next about animals, because they have always been so important to her. She agrees, and thinks it 'might be quite an ASD thing'. She mentions having recently watched a TV programme about Chris Packham, the naturalist and TV presenter, talking about his autism.

'He was talking about the fact that he developed these obsessive loves with certain animals in his life, and I'm totally like that! Do you remember Sherry?'

Sherry was the first horse Alex owned, in her early twenties.

'So I just had this absolute fixation with Sherry. I had her for about ten years. I think the good thing for me, about horses, is being able to be outside. Because I find that very therapeutic. You can understand that when people are depressed, the advice is to go and exercise and to be outside. I always feel that if I didn't have that chance to be outside, and doing things, I think one could get a bit gloomy, so I really like that. I think I've never quite managed to replace Sherry.'

I ask if her sister had wanted particularly to adopt girls. Alex says yes: 'I think Laura wanted girls. I think that was sensible.'

I ask if there is something in her comfort zone there.

'Yeah, totally. I think we are a very female-dominated family. I think our grandmothers were very dominant figures.

'I think it's really interesting, because our mum… she spent our entire childhood telling us to be independent, and have our own bank accounts, and have our own houses, and have our own careers. But there's still an element of, "Oh, why aren't you married?" There's still that conventional... and yet, she spent her whole time telling us not to be conventional.'

Alex says that she also thinks her father, to whom she is very close, would find it difficult if there were other men around.

'He likes to be, you know, the important man around... who'll come and fix the boiler, or gas bottles, or come and buy a car with me, all that sort of stuff. So we are very – I am very – close to him, I think, particularly.

'I think the difficulty for us is although we did grow up with this desire to be less conventional, I still don't think that our generation has quite shaken that off... Because like I said, I'm absolutely gobsmacked by how many young women want to get married, and see that as the be all and end all, and I find that depressing. If that's what people genuinely want... but it's almost like it's just that thing that happens, and if it doesn't happen, then it's weird or wrong. There's no exploration of all the different things that one could do or be. I think, for Lily and Sophia, it will be far more acceptable.'

We discuss the fact that teachers tend to be quite conventional, and small-c conservative, but that they are also faced with the question of how children are gendered today. I ask Alex if she thinks questions of gender are being brought to the fore, and about how she feels the world has changed since we were growing up. She feels there is more discussion than action on the subject of gender identity.

'There are certainly two children I know of that are definitely... have gender dysphoria. One little girl particularly, who just wanted... who would wear swimming trunks and would change with the boys in the boys' changing rooms. And I think that it has to be acknowledged. Acknowledged and accepted.'

Social media is another huge change that has happened since we were at school.

'I think the pressure on girls, and I do think there is a huge pressure on girls and boys to be attractive to one another. You know, sex is still a massive pressure. I think that worries me for

Lily... because she will be exposed, I think she will be fairly easily led, and will probably struggle to discern between positive attention and any attention at all. And also obviously then the question for both of them... they have birth siblings, both have siblings out there, and social media obviously means that it's far more likely that they will be contacted.'

This is one of the complications of adoption – both Laura's girls have siblings who have been placed for adoption in similar families to their own, and some are being fostered by grandparents and other family members. The various siblings will, one way or another, have quite different upbringings, but the urge to locate each other when they grow up will likely be quite strong.

In broader terms, Alex worries about the lack of opportunity for children going through the current secondary-school system. She believes there is a 'lack of really good quality learning experiences. And the opportunity to experiment with meaningful pathways in their life, whether that is through the arts, or through science, or through environmental work, or through farming. I think it's incredibly narrow... There haven't been the high-quality learning experiences that they deserve. So there's no provision for the children who excel in dance, or in art... there is more for sport... but I do worry about the opportunities for those children who are less academic, and those who don't have the family support to help them make a meaningful future for themselves.'

Alex is surprised at how many intelligent and educated women today choose not to pursue careers.

'There's an amazing number of people, though, that I can't get my head round... that I see who are intelligent women who are not in careers – so they're either the stay-at-home mummies in their gym kits, or they're the part-timers who are kind of going, "Oh well, it's a nice, cosy job, and I can do it two days a week," and then not providing the very best for the children in their care. I find that there's an interesting contradiction.' For Alex, a dedicated and child-free career woman, it is difficult to imagine why some women would choose to prioritise children and family over work.

Alex thinks she will go on to become a headteacher in the next four years. That is her ambition.

'It's a very tough job though, and I want to make sure that I'm properly prepared, and also have the right school.'

I ask Alex some more about work, and our mothers, and our lives today. Our mothers were and are an interesting mixture of 1970s feminists – whose aim was for us to be fully educated and to go to university – and traditional, married people. What has this feminism delivered, and what has it not delivered, for women today?

Alex says, 'I think one of the terrible things is the fact that women can go on and have careers and succeed and be leaders, but it is virtually impossible to do that and have a family. Because the childcare provision is so poor, and it is so expensive, and I think that is really, really difficult.

'In all walks of life, there is not enough family-friendly policy, structure... so for example Laura can be a university professor. And you know she's lucky to have her job, and it does allow quite a lot of flexibility. But equally some idiot wants her to be lecturing any day between nine and six. Well, if you have young children, that is really, really difficult. And even when you're earning fifty grand... you're still then paying up to £9,000, up to £12,000, in childcare.'

We discuss the fact that my own set-up is different to the norm, in that I am a salaried professional and my husband works freelance and does all his hours of work around the children's school hours. Alex thinks it is still women who pick up the slack. My own husband is a feminist in word and deed – in the sense that he is willing to do more than just pay lip service to equality. He is willing to look after and raise his own children because he believes it is a job that needs to be done properly.

Talking about me, Alex says: 'You are unconventional, you and David, in that you are the breadwinner, and that's really refreshing, because you don't often see that.'

I comment that it's true, but that I'm still the one who has to remember the guitars and PE kits (although my husband does the packed lunches...)! This phenomenon of women working but also taking responsibility for managing the life of the family has been conceptualized as 'the mental load' – women are overloaded by responsibility for planning and decision-making.[75] Mary Ingham had already observed it in the 1970s, seeing women 'dashing out at lunchtime, armed with shopping bags' and who had 'joined the rat race by doubling up on their domestic role'.[76] It is a feature of women's lives that does not seem to have significantly changed in a generation. It feels very familiar to me, but I do wonder, as well, if it is something that primarily affects women who like to be in charge and who find it difficult to relinquish control. If I ignored entirely the guitars and PE kits, my husband and children would eventually figure out a way to remember them.

Alex agrees: 'My boss is very similar, because her husband doesn't work, but she will say that she's the one that has to unload the dishwasher and feed the cats, and make sure they've booked their holiday, because he won't manage to do it. I think she feels very much that she has this big leadership role, and a successful career, but she will say she's also made big family compromises in order to do that, because she felt that she couldn't... didn't have time to meet people. It's very difficult to pair up when you're working long hours. And I think there is still a huge amount of chauvinism out there, and male attitudes that one feels one's constantly fighting against, and a lack of equality in terms of providing good childcare.'

Are there things that would make this easier? I often imagine having an army of cleaners and housekeepers would make my life easier, but I'm not sure it would. It would be another thing to line manage.

Alex thinks about what might help Laura.

'I think if she could have an au pair. An au pair would make her life easier. Or a house husband/wife! That's what my boss says, she says, "I just need a wife!"'

7

Laura

I meet with Laura a few months after speaking to her twin sister, Alex. Laura also mentions the plan their parents had of sending them to boarding school, and that her father could not, in the end, leave them there. School choices were difficult for their parents, who were both teachers in the private sector. Laura says it was hard for them, 'seeing the kind of education we could have had. They'd been to grammar schools, but obviously we didn't have the opportunity to go to grammar schools.'

Laura talks more about their grandparents than Alex did, but less about their parents. Their maternal grandmother had left school at fourteen, at about the time the war started, to work in a shop. One of her siblings had won an art scholarship to a grammar school, but the family could not afford to buy the uniform and she had left school. Laura's grandmother was, as a result, keen for her own daughter, Laura's mother, to complete her education and go to university.

Laura says, 'She went through the grammar school system and my uncles went to secondary moderns. They didn't pass the eleven plus. Grandad, I think, was always very proud of my mum and supported her going to Bristol University, so that was always very important for her.'

Education is an important theme in my conversation with Laura, who like me is a university lecturer. She remembers her primary schooling fondly, in some contrast to our collective secondary schooling.

'It was a nice, low-key, gentle primary school. We had an amazing headteacher... she did lovely things with us, like she had a young ornithologists' club at lunchtime, so we did birdwatching with her! And she also brought in a spinning wheel and taught me how to spin, and she used to let me take the spinning wheel home at weekends, and I used to sit at home and spin wool!'

Laura was a very artistic child and especially remembers doing creative activities at primary school; this matches my own memories of 1980s primary schooling. There seemed to be less emphasis on mathematics and literacy compared to our own children's experience today, and more on playing and creating, writing stories and drawing. Laura remembers cookery, woodwork, drama, musicals, clay, and art activities. The school was traditional, as well, with an old-fashioned summer fête each year, and country dancing.

'It was a really pleasant environment, I think. I do remember playing. I remember breaktimes – there was a row of trees at the front of the school that had very gnarled roots, and children used to bring in their little dolls or Care Bears and we used to play with those in the roots of these trees.'

My own children play in a similar way among the tree roots in their school field, and it shows how much children benefit from the natural environment if schools can offer it. I wonder how many children play in school playgrounds that do not have any trees at all, or any grass, or plants – tarmac playgrounds enclosed by metal fences. In the 1980s and '90s, our own government sold off many of our school playing fields for profit, and the practice continues to the present decade.[77]

Laura says her parents were always supportive of her education, and her mother, who had studied English at university, helped her with English A level. Laura also remembers her mother's creativity – getting involved with making elaborate costumes for school plays, and props, like plaster-of-Paris ice creams. 'She's creative and always had ideas for art things that we did. It was really... of the period!'

Laura's memory of moving up to our secondary school is, by comparison, pretty negative. 'Hideous' is how she describes it.

Just as she appreciated the pleasant physical surroundings of her primary school, with its 'crab-apple trees and flowerbeds', Laura was acutely sensitive to the secondary-school environment.

'I think from the minute I stepped into that school, to me it was just bleak and depressing and... a horrible, horrible school. I just hated it, I really did. I met some good friends and I have happy memories of making friends, a little bit later, but I didn't enjoy being in that school. I had this sense of dread walking into the school down that long, horrible road that took you to the school gates, and I still dream about those weird bits between the buildings, covered over with the walkway, where the lockers were. It was in a funny kind of grid, wasn't it? I often dream about trailing through those concrete walkways from one block to the other block, and just being... ugh!'

Laura found the environment alienating – our classmates used to sit around on the concrete (neither of us recall any trees, although we did have a field in summer) during breaktimes, reading *Neighbours* and *Seventeen* magazines. It seems innocent compared to what children can browse on smartphones these days during break, but, at the time, for a twelve-year-old to be plunged into the grey, pre-teen world of agony-aunt columns and gossip and bitchiness was a huge culture shock.

Most importantly, Alex and Laura, who'd never been apart at primary school, were put into separate houses and tutor groups.

'Complete segregation,' Laura says, laughing. 'I just had this feeling of being completely bewildered and lost. It was an unfriendly environment... there are people we would totally avoid – be aware of them as a presence, but you wouldn't want to go anywhere near them. People who were loud, who were kind of a bit rough... or the bullies, who would holler, and be really in your face. I used to hate going into that girls' toilet, where the French rooms were, because you didn't know who was going to be lurking in there.'

Girls used to smoke in the toilets, on almost a daily basis. Although young people still smoke, I'm much less aware of them starting so young – at twelve and thirteen – like many of our classmates did. I wonder if we also felt alienated as studious children in a robust environment in which social dominance was not reached through academic achievement.

Laura agrees: 'In the sense of the culture of the school, I remember the people who seemed to be celebrated in the school were the sporting types. I don't remember an ethos. I don't remember a sort of moral code, as it were.'

It was not a church school, and it's true that if the school had values, they were not very explicit – and this contrasts with my children's schools today! I think it was quite egalitarian and accepting, but also quite hands-off in approach. We must have come across as quiet and well behaved, no trouble to the teachers – apart from chatting instead of getting on with our sums. But we were not inspired by anyone or anything, at least not in the first couple of years. There were other quiet and studious pupils for Laura to befriend, who were, for her, 'people who were always a bit of a port in a storm'.

One mutual friend we had was Aisha; Laura was very close to her but didn't ever meet up with her outside of school. Aisha was from a Muslim family, which placed something of a cultural barrier between us even though they were fairly secular. Her parents were immigrants from Mauritius who both worked long shifts as nurses, but they were also a little cautious about the world outside their home. They lived quite far away from Laura's family, so invitations to go and play were not forthcoming when we were younger, and meeting up at the pub when we were in sixth form was off the cards. It's difficult to ever know how much of this was down to cultural differences and how much the individual personalities of the parents, but Laura, Aisha, and I would, I think, have liked to spend more time together outside of school. But we all got on well at school, and I did A level French with Aisha. I hugely envied the fact that Aisha could speak Mauritian Creole, but like Laura, I never really saw her outside of school. I tried quite hard to track her down to speak to for this book but couldn't find a trace of her on social media or in internet searches, nor of her family in the local phonebook.

When I ask Laura about puberty and growing up, her answer is the same as everyone else's – that no one seems to have talked much to us about any of it, whether parents or teachers. It was difficult growing into our adolescent bodies.

Laura says, 'I do remember the awful showers after PE, and that being a major thing – everyone trying to get changed without being noticed. I do remember that side of it, just feeling uncomfortable about those things, and it not being very private or conducive to being private.'

It became more challenging for Laura when she left our secondary school and went with her sister to an all-boys' private school for sixth form.

'There was this real smutty humour about sex. Horrible... boys in the classroom would just tap you on the shoulder and show you a picture in a porn magazine. It was just horrendous. That awful kind of... abuse isn't it?'

If it felt violating at a time when young people's access to pornography was quite limited, it is hardly surprising that young women today, in an era of ubiquitous internet porn, often feel uncomfortable coming into themselves sexually.

Laura says that she had wanted to stay at our mixed school for sixth form, but that Alex had wanted to move to the private school, with better teaching and facilities in the arts subjects they wanted to study. They were told that there would be eleven girls going into the sixth form, but in the end, it was only the two of them and one other girl. It was, Laura says, horrendous.

'I think it was a bad decision, to go there. I remember thinking on the first week there, "*What have I done? I've got two years of this...* Being surrounded by adolescent, stupid, puerile, sexist, immature, idiotic boys constantly, and it was just awful.'

I ask Laura if she got on with any of the boys. She really didn't. Alex got on well with some of them and had a few boyfriends.

'I did everything I possibly could in that school just to stay out of the way and be in the library or be in the private study area or be not noticed or be in the art room, doing extra art!'

Things changed for Laura when she decided to apply to Oxford, to study English. They had a young and enthusiastic English teacher who saw her potential and helped her prepare for the application.

As a younger teenager Laura had wanted to be a ballet teacher. 'I'd done a lot of ballet, but I think I knew I wouldn't be a ballet dancer, but it seemed like a nice thing to do, to teach other people ballet. At that time, you could go and do a teacher's course at the Royal Academy of Dance, and I think that was what I wanted to do. My mum, I remember her saying, "I really want you to do A levels. I don't care what else you do, but you must do a post-sixteen qualification."'

Laura thinks her mother was right to advise this, and I also recall having conversations with Alex and Laura along the lines of always wanting, as women, to be able to make a living for ourselves. We'd seen how our own grandmothers had been limited to the roles they had, whether working or middle class, and we wanted to know that we could support our families and ourselves, if we had to. Likewise, Laura's mother had always worked, and she wanted her daughters to be financially independent. She has succeeded in this aim on both counts. But this didn't mean that Laura had a clear idea of what she wanted to do, aside from becoming a ballet teacher. 'I had no sense that I was academic, absolutely none at all, or that I had the brains to go and study an academic subject. I just wasn't thinking along those lines at all.'

Laura doesn't think there was much emphasis on the more academic children when we were at school. We weren't causing any trouble, and the teachers were happy enough with our progress.

Laura remembers a chemistry teacher once trying to encourage us girls to do chemistry A level: 'The fact she had identified that maybe we would be capable of doing it was interesting.' But we didn't take it further, since we all preferred humanities subjects. We did multiple-choice questionnaires that would produce job suggestions ('window dresser', 'librarian') based on our preferences, not on our abilities. But, as Laura points out, 'there was nothing that said, "Oh, why don't you think about going to university and entering a profession?"'

I don't think we had much sense at school of what 'the professions' were. We knew what teachers did, and we didn't much like the look of it. But where we lived was an affluent part of the country, despite many of our classmates hardly being privileged, and the children of those who worked in 'the professions' like medicine, engineering, the law, or banking and finance, on the whole, attended private schools. The careers advice we received was based on directing young people into skilled jobs rather than professions. It was different to parts of the country where large numbers of young people were funnelled into manual work with big local employers, like factories and ports. There was no heavy industry where we lived. These were, of course, in decline elsewhere by the early 1990s in post-Thatcher Britain, but in the Home Counties, we were insulated from the worst of the economic fallout.

Laura mentions a recent TV series, *Back in Time for School*, about school through the ages.[78]

'It was interesting when they got to the 1970s and '80s and the comprehensive system, and expectations of children, and discipline... and just that there weren't very many really. Not very many opportunities or high expectations.'

Laura remembers certain teachers being kind and enthusiastic, but not ever being pushed to achieve highly. Ironically, she has no recollection of enjoying studying English before sixth form.

There are advantages to this kind of under-enthusiastic, underfunded education. There was literally no pressure on us, so we did not get particularly stressed about exams – not until A levels came around and our university places depended on our grades. Even then, we generally knew what grades we were likely to get. Because the stakes were quite low, there was little competition between pupils and the environment fostered self-motivation. Some of the colleagues Laura and I now work with in universities, who went through the competitive grammar-school or independent school systems, were left with the feeling of having been squeezed through an exam factory, in which grades and university were sole ends in themselves, and with no sense of where higher education would take them later in life. We might have felt a little overlooked, but we were allowed to do whatever we wanted, and some of us took responsibility, early, for our learning. Our teachers seemed to like us if we were good, and they trusted us to get on with our homework, but they were also limited by the resources available to them and they knew there were other things going on in our lives.

Laura gradually worked out that she loved English literature, and that she was brilliant at the subject. In spite of the difficult environment, her new private school had the advantage of an inspiring English teacher.

'He was a good teacher who had read English at St Andrews, and he was a very spiky, intellectual, and inspiring teacher.'

This new teacher was challenging and demanding in way that Laura needed.

'I remember being set a poem by Seamus Heaney to do a practical criticism on and not knowing where to start, and then sitting with my mum and talking it through with her, and then writing up the discussion that I had with her and handing it in. After this piece of work, Laura's teacher encouraged her to apply to Oxford to read English. Laura started to read a lot of Modernist fiction – Virginia Woolf and E.M. Forster – and although she was not formally trained up to sit the entrance exam, she 'had a teacher who was interested in giving me books and talking about books with me', which was as good a preparation as any. She was taught in small groups at her new school, which she feels prepared her well for the Oxford tutorial system of teaching.

Laura applied and was offered a place. I remember her sitting the entrance exam and telling me afterwards she'd written twenty sides of one of those A4 exam booklets in three hours – and her handwriting is quite small. We thought she'd probably get in just based on that.

'I was thrilled about that, and I really, really wanted that. I desperately wanted to go. And I'd also wanted to go to that college in particular – I chose a women-only college.'

Most of the single-sex colleges at Oxford and Cambridge have now become mixed colleges, which Laura regrets.

'I think it's a real shame, to be honest. I really do, because I think there aren't very many places where women can study and work just alongside other women. Without the competition – which is maybe normal and healthy – of having men around. Without that, it's just a very different atmosphere, I think.'

Laura thinks an all-women college was the right place for her to be, but she did find the first year a big step up.

'I found the first year really hard at Oxford, and I had massive imposter syndrome. I'll probably never lose that, but then I enjoyed the second and third year, because I'd taken the special period literature option by that point and just was very excited. I was very excited about the past, and choosing to do a part of the discipline that I didn't really know existed before I went to university. I'd been so, I suppose, conventionally interested in early twentieth-century literature, or nineteenth-century fiction. I didn't know anything more than that!'

Laura spent a long time at Oxford and completed an undergraduate degree, master's, and DPhil there, as well as a temporary lectureship, before taking up a permanent academic post at another elite university in the North of England, where she now lives. We discuss the pros and cons of an Oxbridge education. Laura didn't feel totally prepared for it.

'Even though I'd been to an independent school in sixth form, I still felt that I didn't have the polish or confidence of the people who'd been through an independent schooling. I was still very conscious of coming from a background where there wasn't a lot of aspiration. I was alongside girls who'd been to Roedean or Cheltenham Ladies' College, and St Paul's Girls – really academic schools – who'd done Latin, and they'd done Greek, and a modern language, and they seemed to just be streets ahead. I felt I had to put in such a huge amount of work. I witnessed my immediate peers at the college spending most of their time doing drama, putting on plays, and I would think, *How can you do this? Because I can't – I've got to try and learn this grammar! I don't know how to do it; I don't know how to be confident and easy with it all.*'

Laura recognizes that some of this was just a clever projection, the veneer of competence that an elite education gives young people.

'In fact, the people who did come from the private system ended up not doing that well really, because they didn't work hard. They were relaxed enough and confident about themselves, enough to just do what they wanted at university, which wasn't always necessarily academic, and they just kind of got through and came out with 2.1s.'

Laura attended Oxford in a slightly different era, when not coming from a 'traditional' Oxbridge background, via a famous public school or grammar school, was more unusual than it is today – although there have always been people from modest backgrounds who've gone there. Before our generation, these were more often the grammar-school children, and until very recently tended to be drawn from the best comprehensives and selective state schools.[79]

Laura felt there were gaps in her general knowledge – languages and how to learn them, and the classics.

'We had a very old-fashioned lady teaching us Old English in the first year who had been taught by Tolkien! She was retired really, but she was wheeled in to do Old English classes. And she just expected that we had German and Latin, and I just didn't know how to deal with the grammatical terminology around language-learning.'

Laura and I did actually have a year of Latin lessons at our comprehensive school, but we struggled to grasp things that later on would seem so easy. We were children of the no-grammar generation – in theory, we were supposed to pick up English grammar intuitively, which all speakers of languages do, but it caused some problems when trying to learn a 'dead' language.

Laura says, 'We didn't learn subject and object and indirect object in English, so how could we do nominative, accusative, generative, dative, ablative, vocative in Latin?'

Laura had to work hard at her Oxford college to acquire the necessary knowledge.

'I had to struggle to pull it up… I was burnt out by the end of my first year, because I worked myself into the ground trying to catch up with all these polished young women.'

It did pay off, because Laura achieved a very high first-class degree, and says, 'Yes, I feel privileged to have been there… to have gone through that system and had the conversations I've had with tutors... it was wonderful I think. I feel so grateful for having had that, because I wouldn't have enjoyed the system I teach in now. I don't think I would have flourished in that as an undergraduate. It's impersonal really. That's how higher education is now. You've got classes of twenty, limited office-hour time.'

Laura says that academics now are expected to shoulder heavy administrative burdens while also paying attention to their research careers. In the past, large admin jobs were well remunerated, but it's no longer the case. 'In the system we're in now, you're supposed to divide your time between teaching and research and admin, and there is no prize for doing admin! It takes up so much time and it's the worst bit of the job. It just takes away from your teaching and your research.'

In this context, having been an undergraduate at Oxford during the 1990s, before the era of Big Admin, feels like a privilege indeed.

I ask Laura about her family now. She's still very close to her twin sister, Alex, who lives nearby, and to her parents, who live further away on the south coast. Laura has two daughters, Lily who is nine and Sophia who is five. They are both adopted, and are siblings through adoption. Both the girls had been taken into care at birth and were fostered for the first year of their lives. They were both adopted by Laura between the ages of one and two. How did she come to the decision to adopt?

'Well, I think I always really, really wanted to have children, which is strange when you think about all the other things we've been talking about, and I haven't done anything conventional that leads to the having of children! I haven't got married; I haven't been searching for husbands. I've chosen to do a job that is sort of cerebral, isn't it, and not domestic? I suppose I got to the point when I arrived here, getting a permanent job, and thought, *Well, I've got a job that gives me security financially. What am I going to do?* Because I was in my early thirties, and that's the point, isn't it, where people are often thinking about having children. I think I decided then that I didn't want to go down the sperm-bank route, for lots of ethical reasons. I just didn't feel it was right for me, although I don't feel like it's wrong for anyone else to choose this, but I didn't feel that it was right for me to think, *Oh, I really want a child, I'll go and create one*, when there are lots of children who don't have a family and do need one. I think I'd always been aware of adoption because of having a younger sister who was adopted out of the family, and I'd always been quite curious about adoption, for that reason.'

Laura didn't want to miss out on having children because she had not met a partner who was in the right place at the right time, so she decided to have them regardless. She looked into fostering and respite fostering but quickly realized she wanted something more permanent, so was encouraged by her social worker to look into adoption.

'Then of course you discover that social workers are not anti people being single! Lots of adopters are single people now. It took quite a long time because they were massively under-resourced and disorganized, and struggling as a children's service. I was assessed for a child age three to five, and that was the age group I was preparing to take. When I was actually approved at a panel, they said, "We'll approve you for age three to five, but would you be prepared to take someone younger?" And I said yes, and then the first profile I was sent was this eleven-month-old baby called Lily.'

I ask Laura what it has brought her, being a mother to these girls.

'Well, it's funny, you learn lots of different things about yourself, don't you? I've learnt that I'm not as patient as I thought I was, and not as nurturing as I thought I was! In some ways, it's a lot harder than you could ever possibly imagine. With all those frustrations, and exhaustion and the endless worrying, struggling to get what you think the kids need or deserve, particularly through educational help, or whatever it is. It's just a battle, but I think apart from that, it has brought me what I wanted! Which is to have two children and a family and lots of nice things that you do with them, and I think having children opens up a totally different world. And some of that world is pink plastic crap and the threat of Disneyland… but it allows you to do lovely things that you don't do if you don't have children. You know, it might be looking at lambs or pressing flowers, or going to see a children's play at the theatre. There are those little things which are lovely to do with them. And then unfortunately you realize that the idyll of baking with your children and doing art with them is enough to make you want to rip your hair out!'

I'm a little surprised to hear Laura describe herself as less than patient and nurturing, though I'm sure her children test her limits in the way that all children do. Just looking from the outside, she has provided a calm, safe, and secure upbringing for these two girls. She has a warm and welcoming home that also houses a menagerie of dogs, cats, chickens, and all manner of other livestock. The girls' aunt, Alex, also has a horse and a spaniel that both girls adore. It isn't always easy, and it isn't always harmonious, but the love and security is constant. What is lacking, it seems to me, is appropriate support for adopting parents from social services. Since Laura's girls are perceived to be doing well, it's a constant struggle for her to access the support she needs, especially financially, for them – whether it's play therapy or educational interventions.

The injustice of this situation affects single adopters more than couples. The current wisdom of the government is that child benefit starts to be reduced once one parent earns above £50,000 and ceases to be payable at all above £60,000. Never mind if you are the sole parent of two adopted children who would otherwise be in the care of the state. Never mind if you are paying a substantial mortgage to buy a modest house and household bills on your own, and don't have much left over at the end of the month to cover the costs of meeting the additional needs of these children, and when support to cover those costs is not forthcoming from any other agency. But Laura is keen not to dwell on these issues: this is, ultimately, what adoption is. You become this child's parent, and you alone are responsible for bringing them up.

I ask Laura what would make it better for her as an adopting parent.

'I think, basically, adopters need proper support through access to highly trained professionals – easy access to people who are going to support their children through the kind of emotional issues, social and educational issues. I think that is just completely not there. It would be good, I think, for single adopters to have some kind of financial support. I think what's needed is a proper post-adoption service.'

Laura has experienced a complete lack of continuity with social workers, or social workers who can't do anything for you, 'except perhaps suggest a book you can read, or invite you to a family picnic in the summer'. Services that she had been promised would be available to her after adoption have been defunded or discontinued; the adoption agency she went through folded, taking away some of the support she had. There is nothing in place now for her that can make a difference. But her rock in all of this is her sister, Alex, who lives nearby and who is closely involved in parenting the girls.

In the context, Laura is grateful for the secure employment she has.

'It makes you appreciate the job, and I think you go into work for a rest! I think, *Ah, I've got them to school, I can sit down!* I've been very lucky, I think, to have two children who basically are very healthy and don't have very many problems in the great scheme of things.'

I comment that Laura has approached this situation with a solid and unwavering confidence, that of total acceptance of whatever these children are, and the deep conviction that she is just going to raise them, whatever that brings. It's almost a vocation for her but an understated one, and one for which she asks no congratulations.

She agrees: 'Yeah, I think I probably did have that. That this was what I was going to do, that's it.'

Laura has approached it with the same quiet single-mindedness that she has to studying and securing an academic job. Neither was straightforward, but she did it.

'I probably didn't think enough about the practicalities, as a single parent. The difficult things are like realizing that you've run out of milk or Calpol and you can't easily pop out to get those things. You can't say, "Oh, this weekend I need to finish that piece of work, so the other partner will have the children for me," or, "I need to go to a conference, or I need to go to a research library" – those things are hugely difficult. But at the same time, I know I really enjoy the work I do, but I'm not hugely ambitious about doing any more than what I do. In our job, it's important to focus on the things that you think are valuable.'

Laura feels there is too much emphasis on research impact (which is difficult to quantify in the humanities) and public engagement at universities now, which has certainly been driven by a corporate mentality that has arisen since the introduction of higher fees. She thinks it is valuable to do the work she does, but she doesn't feel convinced that she is going to be changing the world any time soon, nor that she will be heading up large research teams with massive funding grants behind them. What she does is still lone-scholar work, in dialogue with other scholars, but nothing about it has huge societal impact beyond feeding through general knowledge about our own literary culture and heritage, to students and the interested public.

I ask Laura what she thinks has changed between ours and our mothers' generation.

'In terms of the differences between my life and my mum's life, there hasn't been an expectation that I get married. I think for my mum that was an issue at home – who will you get married to? I think my grandparents wanted her to have a profession, and encouraged her to be a teacher because it was a steady and good job. But I think she would've quite liked to have gone into something more arty.'

Planning out a life and career was complicated for our mothers in the 1970s.

Laura says, 'I think my mum has said that when she was planning a family, it was expected that she give up her job really.'

Laura's mother did go back to teaching, but there was no maternity leave, and no expectation that you could go back to the same job.

'She said she wasn't even pregnant, but she realized she wanted to start a family, so that was the time to give up her job. That's astonishing, isn't it? I really hope that the girls have a kind of freedom and opportunity to choose what they want to do and how they want to live their lives. What I'm more optimistic about is that I think there's a lot more freedom about the kind of relationships that you have now. I think there was a lot of... homophobia really.'

Laura does worry though about what she calls the 'vulnerable element' of her girls.

'Those things keep you awake at night, don't they? Drug abuse and... that kind of thing. They do have to overcome the obstacles that are always going to be there... their past. The reason they are with me is always going to be there, and it depends how they respond to that, and how much they can move away from that, or whether they're pulled back towards their past a bit.'

Laura believes all children are affected by their early-life and pre-birth experiences, and that these were, for her girls, less than optimal – despite all the love and security they have received from her since the early months of life. Her eldest daughter struggles more in school.

'You can see she's a perfectly bright individual, but school is not good, really, for her, and it's very difficult to get school to understand.'

In terms of her future, Laura does wonder 'whether in twenty years' time, will I be teaching Shakespeare to a class of undergraduates?' She feels lucky to have a job at a good university and tries, like me, to detach herself from the corporate element of it.

'I know universities are always looking at how we can use our research to make them money, and dress it up in, you know, sort of grandiose terms. I'm just not interested in that. I do enjoy it. I do like teaching; I like my work. I've got projects that will start to take shape once I've finished the last one, and I think I'll just carry on doing the things I'm interested in.'

Times are difficult for scholars in the humanities right now: as I write, the University of Leicester is closing its well-established

English Language and Medieval English programmes; Sheffield is closing Archaeology.[80] The justifications given are often cynical. At Leicester, ceasing to study the distant past is being justified in the name of 'decolonizing the curriculum'; no matter that many of the texts studied predate the colonial era as currently understood. Laura finds this difficult since she sees the Medieval and Renaissance eras as an outward-looking period of rich intercultural and linguistic exchange, given the influences coming from Europe all the time.

I ask Laura about how questions of gender, sexuality, and gender identity are playing out now at university. This is an issue that has developed significantly since our conversation in 2017–18, but at the time we are speaking, Laura feels that tackling these issues in universities is a positive thing, and she's on the equality and diversity committee. I guess Laura herself has felt somewhat outside of the norm, in a minority of sorts, as a single woman in academia.

'I just feel like suddenly this has come and suddenly we've got it! I'm forty-three and we've got it. And I feel ashamed I didn't fight for it more myself, you know? It's not just about the curriculum; it's about how we treat our students, it's about how we use language in the classroom, about how we appoint people, what our staff looks like, and how we treat people of different sexualities, ethnicities, beliefs…'

Laura and I would both describe ourselves as feminists, but I'm struck by how many younger women refuse that label now. It seems to come from an era that is not their own – and they are laying claim to their era in ways that are sometimes surprising and difficult for us. I personally find it difficult to teach students about feminism and gender and sexuality anymore, since it has become such a toxic area for discussion – a minefield, in fact. I feel that womanhood is being stretched as an idea at the same time as it is being emptied of meaning; equally, we are losing sight of the fact that being female is a uniquely vulnerable position to be in, in certain contexts, and something that has produced unique types of oppression. But Laura is more positive than me.

'I feel optimistic about the future and a greater understanding of diversity. I think the student body – women, young women – really struggle with feminism and the pressures on them, in still a very patriarchal society.'

In terms of how things are different for our daughters, Laura feels that the world is, in some ways, more gendered for children than ours was. She says that the presence of the media, and particularly social media, in children's lives is quite invasive.

'Lily is much more interested that I would have been at the age of nine in what she looks like, what she could look like. And I don't know whether that comes down to personality, or whether it's the environment, or what it is, because I'm not painting my nails or anything! … And talking to Alex about the attitude of boys at school, she says they say things that I can't believe boys are still allowed to say, or think it's okay to say to girls… You know, what they want girls to do with them. In the last year at primary school, she's had a lot of problems with boys saying things that are really inappropriate and have sexist and violent connotations. It's still there, and that's depressing, because I think back to my own schools, to that constant chipping away at women and sexualizing women and making women feel bad about how they looked, telling women they're not worth much. That message, to me, has just been broadcast loud and clear by so many voices through my school life, and professional life as well. So I do feel happy now that we've got this recognized committee in the school that is about equality and diversity. I think that's amazing, but it's also extraordinary that it's happening now, when I'm forty-two, and I've been in this institution for ten years and been in academia for nearly twenty years.'

8

Alison

It's a warm, late summer evening in 2018 when I drive to Alison's house to record our conversation. We were in the same tutor group at school, and we got on well, but we weren't close friends so we lost touch a long time ago. She has now moved away from London and lives in a rural market town in the Midlands. She and her husband, Dave, were keen to escape the noise and busyness of the suburbs for a quiet, peaceful, and innocent sort of place where they could bring up their four-year-old son, Leo.

Alison grew up on the same council estate as Emily, Kate, and Kim, with her mum, dad and siblings. She had a much older sister, who had left home by the time Alison started secondary school, and a foster sister. Alison's parents had cared for a few children over the years, and one girl in particular had stayed for a long time. She says the commuter town where they lived 'was a small village at the time... everybody knew everybody'. Alison's home life was more secure and settled than Emily's and Kate's had been – she had more conventionally caring and concerned parents, where Emily and Kate have both alluded to the experience of bringing themselves up.

Growing up on the estate seems to be important in the friends' collective memory, linked to feelings of community and closeness, to commonality of experience.

'We grew up on a council estate, don't know if that's relevant, but it's true. My friends now, that I'm still friends with, were friends that I had when I was little and grew up with, such as Emily, my other classmates that you know… And I had a nice childhood. I never felt I missed out on anything. My dad worked for British Airways, so we went on quite a few holidays – we were quite lucky where that was concerned.'

Alison's father, who worked for an airline, was able to buy discounted plane tickets for the whole family, and one of my first memories of meeting her in second form, the year we started secondary school, is of her telling us about a family summer holiday to America they had just taken. Alison didn't brag about it, but her excitement about visiting the US was infectious, and we were all fascinated: most of us didn't travel much until we were older. The first time I went abroad was a camping trip to France when I was eleven, and many people didn't go abroad at all until near adulthood. But package holidays to Spain and the Greek and Balearic Islands also became affordable in the 1980s and were popular among families we knew.

I ask Alison about her dad's job.

'He was just a baggage handler. I say "just" a baggage handler, but there was no "just" about it! … And he worked for BA for twenty-five years in the end.'

Along with the central importance of the council estate in their memory, Alison and her friends share the idea that they and their parents had modest lives and did not expect more than that: 'I just had, I don't know, a normal childhood.'

What was it like growing up on the estate?

'It was lovely. We could go out and play in the street, and we had a little park opposite where we lived, so we always used to play there. There was quite a lot of freedom. Our parents were happy for us to go out and play. It was what you would want for your children, which was certainly what I'd like for Leo really, which is why we moved here. My mum and dad let me out, the front door was never locked, we would just come and go as we pleased, and I was never worried about half the things I think young people and teenagers are worried about now.'

Alison's mum worked as a cleaner, usually in houses located in a nearby wealthier part of the town: 'She worked in quite a few of the houses there, all the rich, bigger houses.' Their family was traditional in many respects. Her mother worked while the children were at school. 'My mum was the main carer, I guess. My dad used to do shift work, so my mum did more of the caring than my dad, I guess. Typical parenting roles really.'

Alison's sister was seven years older.

'She trained to be a nurse, so we've never been close, because she was always that much older.'

There was also their foster sister, Sharon, who was in between the two siblings in age. Alison does not see either of her sisters anymore, for different reasons that she speaks about later.

'Mum and Dad used to foster, and I don't really remember, because it was— I was quite young at the time, and my memory's shocking. So foster children used to come, and I vaguely remember we had a boy called James come to stay with us for a while, and a girl called Katy, and then we had Sharon, and I remember going to the foster home where she was, so she was… oh, how do you say it nicely? Sharon had learning difficulties. But she was perfectly able to look after herself; she was just a slow learner, I guess, is the way I would describe her. She's got children now. Maybe shouldn't have them, I don't really know.'

Alison expresses, on the one hand, the acceptance of Sharon that her parents had extended to her foster sister, but she's also aware that Sharon is vulnerable and has difficulty caring for her children, in the same way her own mother had not been able to cope – the reason she was in foster care with Alison's family.

'Her mum used to come and visit us, because her mum had… more severe learning difficulties and basically couldn't look after Sharon… and we used to have the social worker, and she used to make scrapbooks and stuff. I must have been about seven, I suppose.'

Sharon lived with their family until the age of eighteen.

'I don't really know what happened. Something happened. She kind of went off the rails a bit, and my mum and dad… didn't wash their hands of her; that's not the right thing… they tried hard, but she ended up going to live in a sheltered accommodation, where there was someone that looked after her. They managed to get her into this place, because she just needed a bit of help, and she wasn't taking it from my mum and dad basically. I don't know why I don't remember… whether it's just the way I coped with it? So we loved her, and she… just kind of went off the rails, and I've never really been able to establish a relationship with her. We tried – when she had children, we all tried…'

Alison's older, biological sister had always found the intrusion of both siblings into her life difficult, to the point that Alison's relationship with her has also broken down in recent years.

'I kind of think my sister's always struggled with the fact that I came along seven years after her. And then Sharon came, and she was an extra, if that makes sense? I think she's always been jealous.'

I ask Alison if she knows what motivated her parents to foster.

'I guess they just wanted to help. It's something that I've thought about, but then I don't know – Dave has always been very, "No, I couldn't," but I guess it's just the helping thing. But then if I look back at it, if I think about my parents, I would never have thought they were the type of people. My mum and dad were the strictest where we lived. I was always in first… I would be in bed and I could hear the other kids outside. My dad is much more maternal than my mum – so from that point of view, I find it quite strange that they would ever consider fostering, because they just don't strike me as those… that kind of person.'

I suggest that you must generally be quite giving, and loving, to be able to let foster children go again afterwards.

Alison agrees: 'And making them feel part of your family, I think that would be quite a struggle.'

Regarding primary school, Alison says, 'I don't remember anything bad about it!' She only has vague memories – of uniforms, and classrooms, and the friends whom she still sees.

I ask if she's still close to those primary-school friends, especially those who came up to secondary school with us.

'Close? Um… Yeah, I see Emily regularly. I've never been a pick-up-the-phone type of person – that's just not who I am; we'll go a month or two without seeing each other, and then we'll get together, and it's just normal, it's just like it was yesterday. It's taken me quite a few years to accept that. I've got friends, but I'm not, you know… like you watch *Friends* on the telly! They're always together, and I think, *I need people like that! Why haven't I got friends?* But I'm just not like that.'

This leads us to talk about social media, and the pressure to be communicating all the time. I admit that I feel guilty sometimes about not engaging much with our family WhatsApp group, or with Facebook, but I just prefer to be with people, and find digital connectedness stressful at times.

Alison laughs, as if in agreement, and adds, 'I'm a looker; I'm not a poster!' She describes social-media communication as 'an extra chore… It's an extra task!'

I've noticed lately, though, that Alison has posted a lot more on Facebook – simple stuff, like pictures of her son and family on birthdays, special trips, and updates on what they've been doing during lockdown. (I wrote this chapter during the Covid-19 pandemic, when none of us were allowed to do much travelling or visiting.)

None of this communication comes naturally to Alison.

'I think, *I must phone this person*, or, *I must message this person*, and it's too much! … It's taken me a while to realize that about myself, but I'm alright with it. I'm okay with being that person.'

A few people have said the same thing, that we've reached a stage in life of greater self-acceptance. Alison agrees: 'Definitely, I think it takes you that long… to be alright with things.'

What does she recall about going up to secondary school?

'I remember it being big. A lot of people. I remember having a big backpack full of books! And just trundling around with all these books and PE kits! I guess I found it quite overwhelming. Obviously, I was with Kate and Emily, so we knew each other, and I had that sort of safety blanket.'

Kate and Emily both had older siblings at our school, who tried their best to educate the younger ones on its street code.

'I remember them saying to me, "Oh, don't do this and don't do that," and I was thinking, *Whoa! What's going on? I don't understand!*'

Alison was told to expect a certain amount of hostility from older pupils – people sending her the wrong way round the school and so on.

'I remember I had the map, and I'm still a bit map-obsessed, like when I go somewhere, I need to have a map. I like to wander, but I like to know where I'm going. And I think that comes from going to Highfield.'

Alison mainly has benign memories of the events of her childhood and schooling.

'I don't have negative feelings. I quite enjoyed school. I never really… I don't think I ever got bullied. Maybe I did… but it's not something that sticks in my memory. I remember the bullies – Kelly Mason! I remember her and her gang! I remember them being quite fashionable, wearing a lot of make-up, and they were just… the popular girls, I guess?'

We both laugh at this. Popular with whom, I ask?

'Probably not with anyone! But when you're that age, you think that they're the ones that know everyone, and had boyfriends, and I don't know… I just remember them.'

Our form tutor was called Mr Wilkinson, and – to my astonishment, given that he was already bald with a grey beard in 1990 – Alison tells me that he is still teaching at our school, twenty-five years after we left.

'Kate's girls have just been through Highfield as well, and she said Mr Wilkinson was still there. She's seen him a couple of times.'

Mr Wilkinson was a maths teacher, who used to run a chess club. He would let us stay in at lunchtime, as long as we played chess.

When the question of jobs and careers came up, when we were young teens, most of us would just say, 'Oh, I don't know,' but Alison would say, 'I want to be a mechanic.' It was her dream, though Alison is not sure where it came from.

'I used to help my dad. He used to have an old Ford Cortina… my mum always had the nicer car, and my dad had the old banger. So my dad was tinkering on cars, and I used to help him a bit; I figured that I didn't mind it, that I quite enjoyed it, and I just thought it was something to do.'

When it came to doing work experience, when we were fifteen, Alison's parents encouraged her to do her placement at a local garage.

'I ended up working at a lorry place. You know T&T, the delivery people? And they had me down the pit cleaning out the big grate thing in the middle! They gave me some overalls, and they were like, "Yep, clean that out," so I was scraping this thing out!'

We wonder if a fifteen-year-old child would be allowed to do this kind of work now. Alison thinks not, but I'm not sure.

'No,' she insists, 'it just would not happen! I helped this guy change his brake pads on his car; I remember sitting in the tearoom with them, having lunch, and I just quite enjoyed it! I don't know what motivated me – I don't know where the initial seed came from. I always used to like watching motor racing and stuff like that. I guess I was always a bit of a tomboy. I quite liked sport... I never saw myself, really, as a girly girl. And I'm still not into make-up and hair.'

Alison ended up literally making history with her ambition to become a mechanic. When she left school at sixteen, in 1992, she found out that it was not going to be easy for a girl to become a car mechanic.

'When I left school, I really wanted to get an apprenticeship. So my dad took me round to all the garages in our area – there was a Jaguar garage and a BMW garage, and all of that. And no one was taking on apprentices, other than Dentons. On the application form, it said you needed to have GCSE grades A–C in Maths, English and Science, which is what I was predicted to get, so I did the application form. Then they asked me to go there... I did three days' work experience, and that all went okay. The only thing I noticed was the toilets they had there were only for men, so I had to come into the offices and use the office toilets – didn't bother me at all – and I think it all went alright... this was throughout the summer holidays.'

Alison found out that three people – two boys and herself – had been shortlisted for the apprenticeship, and that Dentons were waiting for their exam results to decide who would get it. Alison did best: C grades in Science, English and Maths. 'The manager of Dentons rang and said, "As far as I'm concerned, you've got the job," so I was ecstatic, as you can imagine.'

Alison also had a college place to do a BTEC national diploma in motor-vehicle studies, and so she contacted them to say she wouldn't be taking up the place as she had secured an apprenticeship.

But it would not be so straightforward.

'Then I got a letter in the post from Dentons, and it just said, "You don't have the job. We've gone with other candidates; we don't think you're suitable."

I think it was my dad actually who came and woke me up, because he'd opened the letter… He was really upset. He said, "I've woken you up because I've got to tell you, you haven't got the job," and he was really— he was beside himself. Then I think they phoned up the manager of the workshop, and said, "Look, Alison's got nothing now. You told her she had this job, and now she hasn't, she's got no place at college, how can you do this to her?"'

Alison's parents contacted the Citizen's Advice Bureau, who put them in touch with the Equal Opportunities Commission, who agreed to take on her case.

'They gave me a solicitor… I went and had a meeting with her office in London somewhere. She said to me, "Why are you doing this?" and I was like, "Well, just, I don't want them to do it to anyone else. It doesn't seem fair what they've done."'

The case was heard in a magistrates' court in a nearby town.

'There were three people on the panel, and I was seventeen, so I had no idea. It ended up being three days, and on the second day, there were journalists in the court. Then Dentons tried to do an out-of-court settlement – they offered me £10,000 and a Ferrari apprenticeship.'

The solicitor explained to Alison that she could either accept the settlement or continue in the hope of being awarded more money. In essence, the case was proven.

Alison refused the offer although she was ambivalent at the idea of an apprenticeship with another garage.

'I said to my dad, "If I go there, I'm not there on my own merit. I'm there because I have to be. They don't want me, so I don't want it." I was thinking about the apprenticeship more than the actual money! That didn't figure at seventeen; you don't really understand what that means, I think. Well, I don't think I did.'

On the third day of the hearing, there were even more journalists in court. Alison was awarded £3,000 for 'hurt feelings', as well as compensation for lost earnings, added up to a total of around £24,000. At the time, this was the highest payout for a sex discrimination case in UK history. Alison describes it as 'quite a strange experience', but she is still glad she did it. She was briefly a local celebrity.

'I remember this woman stopping me in her car. She stopped the car, she got out, she went, "You're the girl, aren't you? You're the girl off the news! I've seen you! My dad won't buy a BMW from that garage now, he won't!" And I was like, "Oh, okay, that's really good?"' Alison laughs telling the story. 'But we had so many people ringing us up, journalists wanting to talk to me. I did a phone interview on *Woman's Hour*, and it was kind of crazy!'

I suggest to Alison that her story is so interesting because she was carried along by events, rather than acting in a consciously 'feminist' way. She agrees and says she did it for one reason only: 'I didn't want it to happen to other people, and other women basically! I've never been a "burn your bra" type, but I believe in what's right and what's wrong. And what they did was wrong.'

Alison was invited for tea with the head of the sixth form college where she had originally got a place, but she also had some negative reactions from members of the public. Her family was sent a letter from a man in the navy.

'It was addressed to my mum and dad, saying, "You've put lots of false values in your daughter. All she's gonna do is get pregnant – it happens in the navy… she's just gonna be another statistic, and she's never gonna do anything with her life," really slagging me off, slagging my parents off!'

Bizarrely, the family were also contacted by an Australian news network, who accused Alison of 'putting people out of work' because she'd got the money.

'So there was negative stuff, it wasn't all people going "yay, well done!"… So yeah, I had my fifteen minutes of fame! That's quite enough!'

These reactions showed that, although we girls had been taught we could do the same things as boys, good old-fashioned sexist attitudes were still plentiful – visibly in Australia, in particular!

Alison ended up going to college and she completed her BTEC national diploma, and then started working at a local garage.

'They needed someone on the Saturday morning, just to make coffees for customers and stuff, so I started working there. It was just cash in hand… and then when I was at college, again, I had to do work experience, so I did it there, and when I came to the end of my course, I went to see them, and I said, "I need a job – will you give me a job?" and they were like, "Yes," and that was it! I worked in the engine shop… and I worked there for sixteen years.'

I ask Alison whether, after working so hard to land her dream job, she was happy.

'I loved it – I really loved it! I specialized in, it was an Aston Martin garage, so I built engines for fours, fives, and sixes, the classic old style, and that's what I did for sixteen years.'

Despite winning her case, and getting a job, Alison never did get an apprenticeship quite like she had wanted. She did go back to college to get her higher national certificate, but 'it was never an apprenticeship, an official apprenticeship, like you would get from BMW'. Alison worked in the same garage until she was in her early thirties, when she decided it was time for a change.

'Then I went travelling with Dave. I'd met Dave, and we'd been together, and I was kind of bored! I kind of feel like I've lived my career life backwards! I did what I wanted to do. We had a drunken conversation one night, and he was like, "Let's go travelling!" and I was like, "No, we should have children really! It's getting to that point!"'

They decided to go travelling.

'The more we thought about it… "Yeah, do you know what? You only live once – let's just do it!" So we went travelling for a year, and then we came back, and I went back to see Martin [her former employer] and he was like, "We kind of replaced you!" and I was like, "Oh, okay!"'

Alison took a job as a caretaker at a local community college, another stereotypically 'masculine' job. But Alison does not feel remotely bothered about bucking gender stereotypes. She does not have anything to prove – like most people, she just wants to live her life on her terms. Alison doesn't seem disappointed to have left behind her years working as a car mechanic – like she says, she has 'done' her career now, and is happy enough just to have a 'job'.

'I had Leo, had maternity leave, and then we came here [to the town where she now lives]. I didn't work for about a year, and then I got a part-time job.'

Alison worked as a filing clerk in a hospital for a while, and now works as a cleaner in a school.

'It's a secondary school, but they do boarding, so I go and clean the boarding house when the kids go to school. My hours are like nine till two. And its term time, and it just fits in. It means I'm home for most of the school holidays. And that's more important to me at the moment.'

Alison pauses and admits that there are some regrets, or a sense of loss in giving up the level of expertise and status she had working as a mechanic.

'I would like to go back. The mistake I made at the time, in hindsight, was that I specialized too heavily in what I did. So that's all I can do. I built Aston Martin engines; I can do it with my eyes closed. But that's then very limiting, to go into other places. And… I haven't really got the fight in me anymore.'

I ask if this is because she fulfilled that dream and now has other things she wants to do – like a ballerina or footballer who achieves their ambitions when they are young, then need to do new things.

'Yeah, I think I went through a period of bereavement, because I was always Alison the mechanic, and that was very much who I was. And not being that person, I do miss it. I did it for sixteen years, so it was a big part of my life. But like you say, you get older, and it doesn't matter much anymore, as much.'

Having achieved so much, so young in an unconventional career, and having financial security, Alison is no longer bothered about pursuing it further.

'I'd much rather be with Leo. Yeah, I'd much rather be a mum… as much as I can, you know? I still like – even though it's just cleaning, I still like the time of going to work… because then I can just get on – because you can't get on with anything when you've got kids, can you?' Alison laughs. 'You try, and it just never happens, does it? They're a pain! Nothing seems to flow as you want it to flow and you can't get stuff done you need to get done! You don't have to then go and get ten snacks, or a drink, or "Can you change the channel?" or "Can you come outside and play in the sandpit?" – "No! I was trying to clean the sink!" So, yeah, like I say, I do feel a bit like I'm living my life backwards.'

I ask Alison about her relationship with her mum.

'I've always found Mum quite strict. My mum's never seemed that maternal, does that make sense? … My mum and dad aren't the best talkers. They were very sort of British, although saying that, I've always been able to… I had a boyfriend when I was fifteen, when I was at school, so my mum overheard me, she took me to the doctors and put me on the pill, so with things like that…'

Alison continues, 'I've always had boyfriends. I've never really had a period from being a teenager to now of being by myself. Which is something I regret… I guess I've always grown up with somebody else. So I've never, I don't know, maybe I've never grown into me.'

Alison feels that having her son, who is now four, has made her question aspects of her relationship with her parents. 'I do struggle a bit with my relationship with my parents, mainly because now I have Leo, and I love him so much! I just want to grab him all the time, and… I never felt that from my mum and dad, and I know they love me, but then I never felt I was lacking… my childhood was not bad in any way.'

I suggest that maybe it's a generational thing, and a hangover from being the post-war generation – that theirs was a genera-tion who couldn't feel things too intensely. I have no recollection of my parents saying 'I love you' when we were children. It's the same for Alison: 'Exactly, same here.' Although we both agree our parents have become a lot more demonstrative in recent years – and just because I don't remember them saying it, it does not mean the love was not there.

Alison's maternal grandad had fought in the war.

'He was a soldier, and I still don't know much about it, but he never talked about it much. When my mum and dad got married, my mum says she remembers that my grandad said to her, "You're gonna get married… you've made your bed, you lie in it." – "If you go and get married then that's it," kind of thing. Which is a harsh thing to say! She was eighteen at the time. She was still a child really!'

Although Alison's parents married young, they had some trouble with fertility, she thinks – although they've never really talked about it. Alison's sister was born when her mother was in her early twenties, and she had Alison around the age of twenty-eight.

'So that was kind of late, and I think my mum had a miscarriage, which I only found out recently. Some things just come out when you're talking.'

The issue of fertility and having children has also divided Alison and her sister.

'My sister and I aren't talking… since I had Leo, she hasn't contacted me since.'

Her sister doesn't have children, and Alison wonders if the problem is envy.

'She had a bad first marriage. He was horrible, beat her up, she went through all sorts… but I've never been close to her. When I got pregnant with Leo, she got more and more withdrawn the more pregnant I got, and I knew she was struggling with it, because she did have a miscarriage, and she was, with her husband, gonna have IVF, and then their marriage broke up, fell apart, so that didn't happen. So I knew it was tough for her.'

Alison's baby was born around Christmas time. Alison remembers feeling so moved by distant family members and friends sending cards and gifts after her son's birth, but she had nothing from her sister, which really hurt.

'She basically ruined the whole, the whole of Leo's birth, she totally ruined it, because it was just one thing after another.'

Alison says that she was very hormonal around the time of her son's birth, and that her emotions were up and down.

'I remember coming home from my mum's house just in the car, Dave's driving, and in the car saying, "I'm so sorry. I ruined our lives having this baby – we should never have had a baby!"'

Alison is laughing telling me this story, remembering the ups and downs of hormones and emotions in the postpartum period, but her point is serious. She's had no contact with her sister since.

'I knew she was having problems, and if she said to me, "Look, I'm not gonna see you for a little while because I'm struggling with this," I would've said, "That's fine! Come and see me when you want, I get it, it's fine, no problem." But she never did, so I've never contacted her since. I invited her to my wedding. She wrote me a page-and-a-half letter, after four years, of how bitter she was, and how we all conspired against her. I wrote her a two-page letter back, saying— I wasn't nasty or anything, because I got my other friend to read it, I was like, "I don't want to be nasty." But she needs to understand that that's not what happened, and mainly for my mum and dad's sake, because it was really hard for them.'

Alison's parents are still in contact with her older sister, but the two sisters' falling out makes life difficult for them. Especially as Alison's parents now live in Spain. She says they are very happy living the expat life, getting to know other Northern Europeans who've settled in the sun.

'They don't come here as much as I think I would if I had grandchildren, but it's their life, and they've kind of lived it, haven't they? So they're entitled to do what they want.'

I ask Alison what it was like for her becoming a mother. She'd felt no great urge to have a baby in her twenties, when most of her friends started families.

'The maternal thing never really kicked in. For me, personally, it was just, "Well, I'm getting older now, if we don't at least give it a go, then it's never…" Yeah, it was never a burning ambition to have children.'

Alison also struggled to relate to her friends who started families young.

'Like Kate, she got pregnant quite young, and I… I just drifted away from her. Because I was going to the pub at the time, I was young and then she couldn't, because she had a baby, so I just kind of drifted away, and… that's something I regret, I must admit. It's a big, big regret… something I feel very guilty about, to be honest, because I don't feel I can rekindle that now. Although I still see her occasionally, and she came to the wedding.

'I certainly wasn't maternal at that age. It was like, "Okay, well I'm just gonna carry on doing what I'm doing," which was really selfish!'

I remark that at that age, if you don't have children, you have no idea how all-consuming it is caring for a child.

'No, and see, that makes me feel worse, because I think, that's the sort of time when you need someone to come round with a bottle of wine, and say, "It's fine! It's okay! You can get through it!" So yeah, that was just, that was pretty shit really.'

Alison had her son in her late thirties. I'm speaking to her when she is forty-one, and he is now four. She had a straightforward pregnancy.

'Birth not so much fun! That was a bit of a marathon, but he popped out eventually! It was twenty-eight hours or something? I didn't do NCT, but I did the, you know the ones the NHS offer you? So I made friends there – people I'm still friends with; I had a nice little group of mummies, but still… it's not something I really enjoyed either. Not that I didn't enjoy it, but… I found, it's quite hard.

'It's such a massive change, and then you turn into this whole other person. Like I remember, when I was pregnant, I remember sitting watching breakfast news… and President Obama had got voted in for his second term, and I just started crying, because I was so happy…'

Alison tails off, because she's giggling so much at the idea that she cried at Obama's election.

'And I was like, "What is wrong with you? What's happening? Come on!" I think because I was older, I struggled, as well, with how my relationship with Dave changed, because… we would always go away for weekends, we would go to the pub when we wanted, and because I'd had that, it was, again, a kind of bereavement thing, of, "Well, I can't do that anymore." You can't even sit down in the evening and watch telly, because there's this thing, and they're there all the time! And it's never-ending! I found it quite hard.'

Alison's story about feeding her baby makes an interesting contrast with Kate's story – her childhood friend, who had her first baby so young, and for whom breastfeeding came completely instinctively. As a slightly older mother, and as someone who admittedly has mixed feelings about femininity and motherhood, it feels unsurprising that aspects of this did not come easily to Alison.

'I didn't get on well with the whole breastfeeding thing. I tried, and it was the biggest… After about thirteen days, I gave up. That was the best decision I ever made, just because I was putting so much pressure on myself, and I still remember the relief of not having to do it anymore, and not feeling I was doing it right, and the pressure you put on yourself, which… is so stupid! You look back on it now, and it's like, "Why? Why did you feel that?" Because you always want to do right, don't you? … I think that's the whole thing. Being a parent is just a big guilt trip, the whole thing! Am I doing the right thing by going to work? Am I doing the right thing by not going to work? Am I doing the right thing by telling someone that I'm just a mum?'

Alison remembers when someone once asked her what she 'did', she replied that she was 'just a mum'. She felt guilty about this too, 'Like I was being, I was inadequate. Like that doesn't have any purpose or meaning, but… it has the most really, doesn't it?'

Watching Alison with her son, who is keen to listen in to our conversation at the end, is delightful – she is so full of affection, and the bond could not be more complete. She has obviously found it in herself, instinctively and in other ways, to mother him. But talking to her, it feels like she might have been equally happy without children. She has embraced it but maybe could take or leave the whole experience – particularly of parenting a young child.

Again, she feels torn between mothering and the loss of a successful career, and the loss of status as 'Alison the mechanic'.

'I felt, "Well that's not enough, is it? I should be something."
Again, it's the whole loss thing. The older they get, I think it gets
easier.'

I want to ask Alison how she feels things are different today,
for our daughters (for it strikes me that all the other women I've
had conversations with have a daughter or are closely involved in
caring for young girls). I end up asking her if she feels glad she
has a son rather than a daughter.

'Yes, I do, because I think… I've always felt more comfortable
with men. And I think that's just because of my job. Like I say,
I'm not particularly a chatty, ring up women, and like "la la la la
la". I feel like when you're with a group of women, that there's
some sort of pressure to talk, to chat. I don't feel that pressure
with blokes – it's alright to be silent. Like, we're getting a puppy,
Leo doesn't know we're getting a dog, and it's a boy dog. We
could've got a girl, but I was like, "I don't want a girl dog!"'

I ask Alison how it felt turning forty.

'It was okay! We went to Menorca, we went away on holiday,
because… I've never been one to do big birthday things. It's just
not me. But it was alright! It's just an age, isn't it? I do certainly
feel, certainly in the past few years, that I don't really care…
anymore!' She laughs. 'Obviously I do care, but you're just not
as worried by so many things. And… you accept who you are.
I never had a problem with the whole forty thing. I do remember being at school and thinking to myself, *When I'm forty, I'm
gonna be married, I'm gonna have kids, and that's really old!* I do
remember having that thought, and now I'm here, I don't feel
any different. I don't feel old, and I know I'm middle-aged. I
guess I think about death a bit more. I think, *God, I've been
here forty years, I'd be lucky to be here another forty years, I could
have less time than… that's gone.* But then I try not to think about
it.'

I ask her what made her want to get married now, after having a child, and many years together unmarried. Alison says it's
'mainly just because – it was more of a name thing, really'.

She laughs. 'This makes me sound really old-fashioned,
doesn't it? But I just wanted to have the same name. I then got

a bit swept up in the whole wedding thing, I guess. I thought, *Well, I'm only gonna do this once – let's just have a big wedding!* But it was lovely, it was amazing. I liked it when I was engaged, because I had a ring on my finger, and it felt okay to be with Leo, and that sounds— I know a few single mothers, and hats off to them, they're amazing, because bringing up a child by yourself, you deserve a medal, as far as I'm concerned. But… I just felt better in myself, knowing that other people knew. That I wasn't…'

It's interesting to me how many women still want to change their names when they marry, and it is an indication of how small-c conservative a lot of people are, and how, in some respects, the concerns of feminism affect many women very little. Mary Ingham talked in 1981 about the difficulty of having the title 'Ms' recognized as an alternative to 'Mrs' or 'Miss'.[81] But today this seems strangely passé. Most women don't really mind the status quo, although I was sure I'd never change my name, even from a very young age.

It seems that there is still some shame attached to being a single mother; Alison is aware of this, of feeling potentially stigmatized, but also the tendency in ourselves to judge others. After all, a lot of her friends have had children on their own.

'That's awful, isn't it? It makes me sound really shallow!'

Alison prefers having the same family name, but part of her is uncomfortable with this convention too.

'I still struggle, and being called, being a Mrs, I just find that – that's so odd! That's another thing that makes me feel old. And I like listening to Radio 2 now, but again, I'm alright with that! I don't care! The Mrs thing makes me feel old, because it makes me think of the teachers at school!'

Alison feels settled now. She has moved around a lot with her husband, who was a builder for a while, as they bought houses and then gradually renovated them before selling up and moving on. They made a bit of money that way, but now she's ready to stop for a while. She's excited about getting her puppy.

'He's a Miniature Schnauzer. I've kind of wanted a dog for a while, just because I can't… We tried to have another child, and it didn't work out. And now that I'm too old, and that's not gonna happen, so I've kind of let that one go, although I've substituted that now for a dog! I like dogs that have character – he looks like an old man! And like I say, it's a boy dog – clearly it's in my comfort zone!'

9

Kim

Kim was born in Wales, to a South African father and Welsh mother, and lived there for the early years of her life. She has three siblings – an older sister and two younger brothers – and the family moved several times when the children were young. Kim lived in Wales until she was six, in 1983, when her father moved the family over to South Africa to live, before returning to the UK in 1986. Kim joined our class in fourth form, when we were fourteen, at the beginning of our first GCSE year.

'My dad's parents divorced when he was two, and his father is Afrikaans. He remarried, had three more children with his new wife in South Africa, and continued to live there. My dad's mum was from Wales, so she moved back to Wales with my dad.'

Kim has an unusual Dutch surname, which is a striking marker of her origins. I ask her what she remembers about living in South Africa in the 1980s, and whether she recalls anything of the political upheavals that were so intensely reported in the British media at the time. But political events don't form the basis of Kim's early memories.

'I think it was like being a kid… We were there for three years, near Johannesburg. It was during Apartheid, which I knew nothing about at the time. I mean, the context of the family is more complex, in the sense that my grandfather – my dad's dad – was in politics, and he was friends with Hendrik Verwoerd, who had designed the Apartheid. So my grandfather was fully fledged in Apartheid beliefs and advocacy. That was something my dad never aligned to, but it was something that had been part of the family, which I only discovered later.'

It is not surprising that Kim and her family didn't talk much about this element of their history. It was a complex experience to be a white South African in the 1980s and '90s in the UK. The government and consumers boycotted South African produce (grapes and apples, I seem to remember) and campaigned for the release of Nelson Mandela. South Africa was a pariah state, so I can imagine that Kim and her family sometimes got a hard time for being, in however indirect a way, part of that.

When we were about ten, in 1986, the popular satirical TV show *Spitting Image* recorded and released a song with the extraordinary title 'I've Never Met a Nice South African'. This became an easy chant for school bullies sniffing out any hint of difference.

Kim thinks the family's association with South Africa was harder to handle for her older sister, who was nearly fourteen when they returned to the UK.

'She was more aware and was in that time of life. Since then, she's used the word shame... that she experienced some shame, coming back to Britain, and trying to represent our lives out there.'

Certainly, they were made at times to feel like outsiders – Kim was singled out for having a Welsh accent, for not being English, and yet she was sometimes considered South African. One way or another, we didn't do a very good job of making sure she felt like one of us.

Kim remembers South Africa as a place different to the political cauldron it appeared to be to outsiders. But she does evoke elements of the life of privilege that white South Africans enjoyed.

'As far as I was concerned, we had family nearby, we'd go and hang out with them, we went to a nice school, had some really nice friends – oblivious! And I continued to be oblivious, probably, for a lot of my life. My memory of South Africa was... it was a good time. It was spacious. There was a lot more land. A lot of playing outside, water – I just remember going to water parks! Just things that were really fun. I think it was active. So, for me in my mind, it literally is a colourful, bright part of my memory.'

On their return, the family lived in Cardiff for four years, then moved to the suburbs of London, which is when Kim arrived in our school. I ask Kim how she thinks the family's way of life, and moving around, affected them.

'I think each of our experiences is different. I don't think any of us has got the same journey. I think for my dad, each of the moves was quite purposeful, and the purpose was caring for our family. Trying to create an environment that worked for us. I don't think that he realized it could have much of an impact, emotionally, on any of the children.'

Kim's siblings have gone on to have accomplished – if unconventional – lives and careers. One of her brothers is a self-made entrepreneur, and her sister has forged a successful career in the music production industry. One thing their parents appear to have communicated to them is an unwavering optimism, a sense of self-belief, and a deep faith in providence.

'Mum had grown up in a little place in Cardiff all her life. She'd never been abroad, I think, until we moved to South Africa, so it was quite a big thing for my mum, to uproot, relocate, find a new way of living. But I think following Dad's lead and wanting to keep a stable space for us as a family, she was up for it.'

Kim appreciates the flexibility this gives her now. Having a young daughter today, 'there is part of me trying to think about where we live and wanting to have a long-term view about where we live. But I also believe that you can switch schools, or switch houses, and build relationships. So I do feel like there is some freedom.'

Going up to secondary school, Kim appreciated the move from a rather permissive primary school in Wales to a more formal high school.

'I actually liked the structure a little bit, because in South Africa, school was much stricter, and my last year of junior school in Wales felt difficult. I remember Highfield being quite musty and dark… the corridors and the classrooms. Almost as if there was a lot of wood and not a lot of natural light. That's the impact on me, so I do remember coming into the classroom, and… I wasn't very inspired!'

Kim became quite good friends with Anna and me, and a few others, during those GCSE and A level years. Without these friends, Kim says, 'I think it would have been a really undesirable few years at school. I think I'm good at going into new environments, and finding connections with people, and socializing, but what I hadn't had before you guys was actually close friendships or that reciprocity. And I think it was being met as an equal person who was respected, but also… just fun, you know?'

Kim lived on the same estate as Alison, Emily, and Kate, but didn't spend a lot of time with them. Perhaps she arrived too late, and the peer groups were already established.

'We'd get the bus together… they would be part of my broader group of friends, because they were in our tutor group, and I sat next to them in various lessons. So there was a connection, and there was a genuineness in there, but interesting, it never developed.'

It didn't feel like a loss to Kim when these friends didn't stay on to do A levels. But she also thinks that, because of all the family moves during her childhood, she's used to making friends and then leaving them behind – almost like a natural attrition.

Adolescence was challenging for Kim because of the natural conflict between the stricter, traditional values of her home and the wider cultural environment. 'I think I did a lot of reflecting on it at the time. I'd got boxes of journals I was continually writing! It's interesting because I feel like I've grown more and engaged more with that area of my sexuality in the last— well, I got married a few years ago, but probably in the five years before that, so really, in my mid-thirties was the time I think I started to unpick it, in the way that a lot of people did in their teenage years!'

Kim thinks that during her adolescence, her tight-knit family was a strong guiding force.

'That overrode a lot of the other pulls, and I think it was a way of me coping with my emerging sexuality and want for a relationship. I think I created an almost ideal of what I thought a man would be, or a boy would be, that I'd want to be with. And so anybody that didn't fit that image, or that ideal, I just didn't give time to. I might have had a bit of attraction or a bit of interaction... but I wouldn't go anywhere with it – even if they pursued me. And when I met someone who, in my mind, reflected some of those qualities or some of that fantasy, then I was very focused and avidly interested in only that person, which seemed to be a pattern through the next twenty years really! And they were never the ones that pursued me! So, in a way, I never really got caught up in, around, exploration with boys, because of this mindset that I had. It served me for a period, because it avoided a lot of complexities. It kept me out of trouble, and I remember being fourteen, thinking, *There's no way I'm going to make it to sixteen and not have sex! Like, my hormones are raging!* At sixteen, *I don't know if I can control myself!* Because of this way I had it in my mind – which was self-imposed; I don't think it was imposed from someone else – it took me, probably, until thirty-five, thirty-six, to trust myself, I think. To open up to other people really.'

Kim did her A levels at our school, and although higher education had never been her expectation, she then went to university in London to study for a degree in nursing. Kim had thought she would do a job that involved working with people, something that 'could just be human and spiritual', before settling down to have her own family.

'My parents hadn't gone to university, my sister didn't go to university, my grandparents hadn't gone to university, so it really wasn't an interest. But I remember the PE teacher we had at school, Miss Jackson, she drove me home one day, because I didn't know my way home, must have got lost or something, after hockey, and she was saying, "Oh, I think you'd really enjoy university." And I was like, "Really? Why?" And I also thought, that's a more intense environment of people maybe engaging in a way of life that I didn't want. Because I was quite clear about my morals, so I was thinking, *I don't know if I want to live with them. I don't want to live with a bunch of drunken, promiscuous people*! But she introduced it, and I didn't have a better option, and everyone was filling in the UCAS forms and stuff.'

Had Kim come of age today, in 2021, she might not have gone to university at all. In the mid-1990s it was a risk-free move. Your fees were paid, and there were also maintenance grants available to students from lower-income families. Would the gentle encouragement of a teacher be sufficient, today, for a sixth-former like Kim to pursue higher education, when she wasn't entirely sure what she wanted to do, and when it would incur taking on debts upwards of £50,000? But Kim did go to university and completed a four-year nursing degree. It was not always easy.

'I wanted to leave nursing about halfway through the course but decided to see it through.' She then worked a mandatory year as a nurse in order to complete her qualification, and worked in nursing for a further two years before taking a conversion degree to train as a midwife. She then worked as a midwife in a London hospital for thirteen years, alongside the same team of people. Kim eventually left midwifery because the service delivery was changing in a way she didn't like.

'When I was training as a midwife, I realized the only place I'd be interested in working was with what they call continuity of care, so where you get to meet the same women all through the pregnancy, and then you're available for the birth, and look after them afterwards. I think the first year and a half I worked there was probably the most satisfying work experience I'd ever done, because I think I was quite sharp from having just finished my training, quite updated on things. And because I'd had the experience of being a nurse for several years before, I think clinically, I had quite a bit of confidence in my own judgement, so I was a novice but not a novice. I gave a lot to the women I was looking after, and they gave a lot back, in terms of appreciation, and I felt very valued in what I was offering... I mean, it was valuable. It was very different to the model of care most people were getting, so I do remember driving around feeling really happy in my car! I was just who I am and this job – it seemed a good fit.'

The rapport with the women she was working with came naturally.

'You know, keeping a peaceful environment in a stressful state, and there was a lot of anxiety that people were in, and I had the resources in myself at the time to be able to support them with that. I think birth is such a powerful experience – it's the lynchpin that the antenatal and postnatal work, service, is around. Doing that whole journey was lovely. But it was exhausting because you manage your own diary. So I'd go from a birth, maybe not have much sleep, but then was trying to follow up with the other people I had appointments with in the day. The difficult side of that, as well, is because you're so invested, and they're invested in you, when there are moments of stress, or if I didn't feel confident, it was quite hard to handle that because… you want to show that you're really good at something, or that people still trust you, or that it's gone well. And when it's not, it's harder.'

All this took a toll, and Kim was quite burnt out after the first year or two. She found that she never quite had the same level of motivation or enthusiasm or resource after that. Kim later decided to train as a life coach and worked in that capacity supporting postnatal women and midwives towards the end of her midwifery career.

At the time of our conversation, Kim's been married for just over two years, and she has a thirteen-month-old daughter, Mia, born when Kim was forty-one. She also has a twenty-four-year-old stepdaughter, who she says is 'more of a friend really'. Kim met her now-husband in 2013, at a personal development course.

'I really enjoyed his company, and I enjoyed him, so I was willing to stay in contact, but I had no intention of anything further. And during my own journey of, you know, I was saying about opening up and exploring stuff, I think I just softened and opened. So, eventually, a year and a half before we got married, it just dawned on me that maybe I loved him! And we were going to meet up just as friends, but I suddenly realized that I was interested in more than that, so I communicated something of that to him. And immediately, it just changed into a developing relationship.'

I ask Kim how it was for her having her first child at forty-one. This does not seem so late these days, as more and more women have babies in their forties, but it is also an age by which some of our school friends had become grandmothers.

'So, just going back, I had thought I'd have lots of children. I'm one of four. My mum got married at twenty-one and got pregnant with my sister almost instantly, so that was my image. I remember being in Wales, before we even moved here, with a view of, "Not interested in studying. I'm interested in family; I'll be married at nineteen. Have four kids." Four to six kids, I actually had in my head! It was complete fantasy! ... I gravitated towards children, and as a teenager there were some families close by that I got friendly with who had young children that I would often go and hang out with. I really loved it, with a view that this would be a part of my life as well.'

But the idea of university planted in her mind by our young teacher at school led to a rethink.

'I think at some point in university I realized that as a young adult, independent, free of responsibilities, I didn't want to live my twenties and thirties living someone else's life and looking after their family. I wanted to have the freedom that I could have... And I think the broodiness side of things just got met by being a midwife. I was always around brand-new babies and families and seeing the stresses and joys of it, and having a valuable contribution, getting to hold babies, so I didn't feel that broody. Also, my longing was so much about having a partner and a relationship – to find somebody that I could share my life with was what I wanted. The desire wasn't like some people I know who said that they wanted to just go down the IVF route, with a donor or somebody, as a single person, because they wanted children so much. I wanted a context for children that I didn't have, so it was almost the second thing along the rung.'

By the time Kim met her partner, she understood that starting the process of having a family was not necessarily going to be straightforward. She was also not wedded to the idea of children at any cost.

'When Andrew and I got together, I really had the sense of, "It's not a dealbreaker for me." I noticed there was still a longing to have children, but it was also something I was willing to let go of, because I was already thirty-nine… I had no idea if I could have children, had no idea if he would want more children – he's ten years older than me – and it was like, I'm willing, I'm holding it lightly. We decided we weren't going to use contraception with a view that we would love to have a child, but equally, we weren't going to go actively down the route of trying to have intervention to have a child – that we were just going to see. And give it a year and see – if I didn't get pregnant, then we'd just acknowledge that maybe that wasn't for us, and we weren't going to have kids. I think some of my friends thought I was ambivalent about it. I think I wasn't ambivalent; I just didn't want to be disappointed. I didn't want to hold too tightly to it. But I did have a hope, and I was satisfied with being a newly married woman! And having somebody that I really loved and loved me.'

Kim got married in June, and in October found out that she was pregnant. I ask her about how the experience of pregnancy and birth went – from the perspective of someone so knowledgeable about it from the other side.

'It was fascinating. I was more anxious in the first few months than I expected, before my first scan, because I knew quite a lot about people having miscarriages that weren't known. I didn't expect that, to have any anxiety, but managed to find a way to get peaceful about it. I had a really good pregnancy, and it was nice, just observing me and observing stuff. I'd always wondered what it was like to have a human being in you, growing and moving. It's strange and amazing, and uncomfortable at times! Also, not working, I got a chance to fully experience it. I could truly just say, "This is my pregnancy." It was helpful because my team of midwives could look after me, so I had people I'd worked alongside that were my midwives, who were there at the birth as well.

'When I was in labour, it went really well. I wasn't scared. I understood the process, and I could use the tools that I had for support. I remember being excited because I had a quick labour… From the first contraction, she was born five and a half hours later, and the midwife was only there with us for just over an hour before she was born.'

Because Kim knew the process of birth, she knew it was going well and the baby was fine and healthy.

'And again, just with breastfeeding and stuff, because I have supported so many people with that, I knew what I was doing. I knew how to handle a newborn.'

Kim has embraced motherhood and all it has brought her. How does she feel her life is different to her mother's, in terms of the era and experiences, and how does she think her daughter's life will differ from her own?

'I think my experience of life has been very different to my mum's. Hers was a lot narrower, both in mentality and exposure. At that juncture of deciding, like, university, my mum had a good conversation with me, saying that she had prioritized family over pursuing something academic. And there were times where she would have been curious to know what it would have been like to have done a different route, and I remember that conversation. It was quite a helpful conversation for me, to know that there was value in freedom, I think, to explore going to university and a wider world. I don't know if she would remember that conversation, but it did push me a little bit, to go wider. In a way, I think my mum's opening up of experiences and life has happened through and after having children, as an older adult, whereas I think I got quite a lot of varied experiences in my twenties and thirties. And actually my world's got a lot narrower now, having a newborn and being more home-based, which works for me at the moment!

'I think one thing is good, and I think Amy, Andrew's older daughter, being around is really helpful, as I think there is more awareness. With Amy, she's insightful and communicative, and has a lot of awareness around gender, about humanity! And an ability to articulate that, and a sense of confidence, self-worth, that I think is more enhanced and more talked about than maybe there was twenty or thirty years ago. I'm encouraged that there are people in Mia's life who have that, and can support her in that, as a person. I think there's a real possibility to thrive.'

I ask Kim what she thinks about the impact of the internet and social media in the lives of young women today, because none of this arrived in our lives until we were in our early twenties, after 1998.

'I think the whole of social media, your cyber image and your human image and that disconnect… It's like I don't really know that world myself, and for Mia to enter it, and it just be a big part of her world, that concerns me, and I don't know how to handle that, but I trust we'll find a way. Also, I think wanting to teach her about things that are substantial, like the inner world… I do want her to have a consciousness of something that's more than just the physical and the superficial and material… an awareness of something that's more. But I don't think that's what's being pushed in the world that we're in!

'And I'm not, certainly not the most politically or socially aware, but we're right in the middle of a time where Brexit's going on. We've just had Boris Johnson elected. We've got Trump in America; we've got the climate-change issues. I don't think I have fully received the impact of how real that is. So I'm in a bit of a bubble right now, of home and family and close people.'

I say to Kim that it's hard to look outwards when you're at that stage; I remember wondering how I was supposed to turn my attention to environmental matters when I had two young children to look after, which took every scrap of my energy. All I could do was care for the things that were right in front of me, right then.

I ask Kim what it means for her, turning forty.

'I think it was significant in the midst of the life change that was happening. I turned forty the month after I got engaged, and I think I've always been quite excited around decade changes, because it always seems quite a significant turning point. It almost seemed like everything was leading up to that point. It was a bit like coming into a new, clear space. I didn't know what it would hold for me, but it felt like the ending of a chapter – it was the convergence of becoming. I was still forty when we got married, and my engagement ring, it's got forty diamonds on it. I think forty was a very significant mark in my life, because of the world that was finishing and beginning.'

10

Natasha

Natasha grew up in a large and vibrant village in the area which marks the end of the suburban stretch surrounding London and the beginning of the wide, rural countryside of the South of England, beyond the M25. For this geographical reason, the village contrasts with the town where I grew up, some seven or eight miles away, and the town in between where we went to school, which were both busier, more polluted, and more suburban. Natasha went away to university in Kent and lived abroad for a few years before returning to live in the village in which she'd grown up, with her husband and two children. She had a career in logistics and then in the charity sector, and currently works part-time, around her children's school hours and holidays, for a local debt charity. Natasha and I had not been close lower down the school, but we became firm friends in sixth form, and we studied A level French together.

The family Natasha grew up in was 'a typical nuclear family. Mum and dad, two children, me and my younger brother. Mum and Dad stayed together; they're still together... they're coming up to fifty years. We moved here in the early '80s – because my dad's job had transferred to London and my mum got a job at the hospital.'

Natasha's mother was a doctor, a GP and later a psychiatrist, and her father a civil servant – 'very middle class!'

Natasha's brother is twenty-one months younger than her, but he is a foot taller – 6'4" to her 5'4". And the differences between the siblings are, in other ways, quite striking.

'Despite the fact that he's my younger brother, he often feels like my older brother. Especially as he had his children a lot earlier than me.'

Natasha's brother married and had children in his early twenties, but she has done these things a little later in life. Their childhood was stable and unremarkable.

'I would say it was a very happy childhood! You have your own children, and you reflect a lot more, don't you? The simple things you remember – playing in the garden. Now I live back in the village, I take the kids to places we played when out in the countryside. I take the kids to the big tree we always went to. It's all the memories I have of childhood, of taking a picnic, of having a happy day out, I guess I'm doing them again, because I loved doing them!

'Coming into teenage years, this village was my hub, so although I was at school at Highfield, I had friends in the village. A lot of my socializing would be around here, just a big group of us going around on our bikes, going around the countryside, or occasionally we'd get the train into London for a wild night! You know, not wild, but it was exciting. But just a very carefree growing up... There didn't seem to be pressures or stress...'

Natasha says she had a lot of freedom.

'Yeah, I guess because I had a mum who worked, so this is from about the age of twelve now, my mum was full-time working. So we got on with our own stuff in teenage years. We just filled out time really. It was very much our group of friends.'

I mention to Natasha a memory I have of her saying she was a 'latchkey kid' when we were at school. She doesn't remember describing herself in this way.

'I have no memory of that! My brother has similar memories, which is interesting, because that has really fed into his parenting. He and his wife have been very, very hot on making sure they're around for the children.'

I wonder whether in fact Natasha had told me that her *brother* thought he was a latchkey kid, that I had misremembered.

'I obviously did talk about it like that, but I think what overrode it was the pride I had in my mum, and what she did, so my memory is probably through rose-tinted glasses. I probably look back and think, well, she was doing a great thing, and these were the consequences – that we lived the way we did. But I don't see anything negative about that. Through my younger years, my mum and dad shared the house – shared everything, I guess. My dad had jobs where he would work from home a little bit while Mum was at work, so there was only one day a week where we had to go to somebody else for childcare, and that was fine. There was always Mum or Dad around.'

As they grew older, the family also hosted au pairs from all over Europe, whom Natasha enjoyed having around.

'When I turned twelve, my mum turned forty – and I remember it because it was her surprise fortieth birthday party – and she'd just got her consultancy post, so we celebrated the fact that she'd turned forty and the fact that she'd just become a consultant, and that was it. Life just flew for her – she just threw herself into her career. And my dad just picked up running the home really. Although he worked full-time, he would go off to work very early and be home by four thirty; he'd pick up the shopping – he'd pick us up from school if we needed picking up late or whatever, or were at clubs. Then we'd come home, and we'd help him cook the dinner, we'd have a meal together, and then Mum would come in about six, maybe seven o'clock, and then I just remember her sitting on the sofa, eating her tea before she then launched into doing more work of an evening. That was just how it was.'

You get the sense talking to Natasha that her parents, unusually for the era, were equal partners who took joint responsibility for home and family matters – they were pioneers in terms of gender equality, but they were also making it up as they went along.

In the 1980s and '90s, it was still more common for middle-class mothers to stay at home or work very part-time, and for fathers to work long hours in careers. But Natasha feels that, despite these commitments, the family did ultimately always come first.

'There was always a long family holiday in the summer. We'd always have three weeks together. Mum was around at weekends.

I think my brother felt it more than me because he was younger than me. I was quite academic and applied myself to my studies, so that meant I related to my dad really well, because that had been his way out of poverty – his education. He'd come from a very working-class background, and through getting into grammar school, he'd escaped all of that. So from when I was just happy doing my work and studying and interested in all of that, I just kind of got on with it.'

Natasha is curious about my 'latchkey kid' memory. Had she said it to be negative about her family's way of life? I didn't think so. We decide that as teenagers we probably discussed our respective households and parents' approaches to the home. Natasha remembers that my home was an open house, and that I never possessed a key to it. This was true.

But Natasha reckons that some girls had closer relationships with their mothers than we did.

'I guess I didn't have that cosy sitting around chatting with my mum thing. I knew that other people had it. I knew there were girls that were talking about going home, sitting with their mum and having a cup of tea and talking about their day, and I just knew I didn't have that. But I knew my mum would drop everything for me.

'I'll never, ever forget the day of my A levels, when I came to school and I hadn't got the grades I wanted to go to Nottingham University, and I phoned her in floods of tears – "I haven't got the grades!" And she just said, "I'll be with you; I'll be there." She was in a meeting, and she just said to them, "I've got to go. My daughter needs me!" And she left everything, and we went and had a day out at the seaside together, and to me, that meant everything. Because it indicated to me that I did still come first, but it does suggest that there were lots of other times where I would have wanted her around, but she wasn't, and I just accepted that.'

But as a role model, Natasha says, 'I just think it was amazing – and empowering! I remember talking to the deputy head one day at school – I think it must have been in the sixth form – and saying, "My mum's a consultant psychiatrist." And he went,

"Oh, well, she must earn a lot – she must earn about £40,000!"[82] And I was like, "Oh, I guess she does!" I didn't have a clue! Because we didn't talk about money in my family, but I thought, *That sounds like an awful lot of money.*'

Natasha's mother would have earned more than her father, and clearly our deputy head was impressed given 'the way that he sort of puffed up... because of what she did! Yeah, I was very, very proud.'

It's clear to me that Natasha wasn't proud because of the family's relative wealth, but because of what her mother, as a woman of her generation, had achieved.

Natasha's family, with two full-time professional salaries, was probably one of the wealthier ones in our school. But they seemed pretty ordinary – they lived in a nice, detached house (where they still live, after forty-plus years), but it's not fancy. There was nothing ostentatious about them. They didn't seem at all materialistic to me – there were no status symbols or obvious markers of wealth, like cars, which were common then as now in the Home Counties. They had holidays in France, but they'd stay in rustic *gîtes* rather than hotels. They were comfortable and didn't need to worry about money, but they didn't flaunt it either.

Natasha's mother was a formidable role model for us, as Natasha's friends, to have around. I only met her a few times, but she made quite an impression. Her path was certainly an unusual one, since medical schools in the 1960s still operated quotas that advantaged young male students.[83] Her mother had a relentless optimism that Natasha has inherited, and projected utter self-belief and competence. But she was also down-to-earth, practical, kind, and funny. These were traits that people of her generation didn't always communicate to us as young women coming up in the world.

Natasha sat the eleven plus for a selective girls' grammar school in London, but she didn't pass it. Her parents then decided our school was a better bet than the nearby comprehensive. Today, the schools' reputations are reversed, and Natasha says her children will go to the local school, not Highfield, with its more dubious reputation.

She has good memories of school.

'I think it was positive, to be honest. I was stretched enough academically. I felt like I had a lot of opportunities, like I loved doing things like drama. I loved how, by the time we got to A level, we had smaller classes and we had those lovely teachers – especially in French. I made some lovely relationships. And history was similar. We had those young teachers we all fancied! I wasn't very sporty, so I wasn't pushed – that was brilliant! ... Do you remember cheating on cross country? [I do.] Do you remember we all got caught? They used to stand in the middle of that shortcut and catch us!'

Natasha was the sort of pupil every teacher wants to have in their class: smiley, optimistic, bright, hard-working, and kind. She was in charge of creating the yearbook in 1994, when we were in upper sixth. But these are not the things that confer status in the comprehensive school environment, at least not in the first few years when the tough kids rule the school. If we misbehaved, we were issued with blue 'misconduct slips' (or yellow for 'serious misconduct'). The disciplinary system was understood.

Natasha, who wasn't a natural rebel, recalls, 'I remember the first year, desperately trying to get a blue slip, because I felt like I hadn't been naughty at all and I needed to obviously do something, so I did things like forget my apron for CDT [craft, design, technology]. The teacher said, "It's alright, Natasha! That's okay."'

Natasha eventually managed to get one for 'forgetting' her French book, but it had been a real effort. I, on the other hand, got a lot of blue slips even though I desperately wanted to be good, because I felt I was naturally bad.

'You were deeply bad,' Natasha says. 'I was deeply, boringly good! Trying to please everyone, which I've been trying to undo for the rest of my life! But, I mean, that's just me.'

In second and third form, Natasha initially got in with a group of girls who later excluded her – a particularly cruel, usually female, form of bullying.

'Those girls turned out to be very into relationships – sex, that kind of thing. I think, I don't know.'

This was when we were fourteen. Natasha was not yet into boys, or interested in sex, at this stage and so distanced herself from the group.

'I got in with another group of girls who were like me, just serious about studying, and boys… you just had fantasies about them really. And then when you hit fifteen, sixteen, you'd go to parties and snog somebody, and that would be all the excitement you wanted really!'

There does seem to have been a class element to our sexual development. For some reason, those with middle-class parents seemed to be encouraged to stay young and innocent for longer – perhaps preparing us for the years of study ahead, and to prevent us from making life-changing decisions too early in life. It has, perhaps, ever been thus. Mary Ingham noticed it too, when she was at grammar school in the 1950s:

> The council estate girls were all going steady at thirteen, setting their hair in rollers, wearing natty suits and lipstick and stockings, and generally flaunting their femininity long before my friends and I did.[84]

Natasha wasn't ready for the lipstick and boob-tube element of mid-adolescence, so once she distanced herself from the girls who were experimenting with sex, she was more comfortable.

'I was scared of the girls I was scared of, but then I had enough friends. I didn't particularly enjoy the fifth-form ball. I thought that was horrible.'

We wonder now why we put ourselves through it. The pictures from the yearbook reveal that we were still in the 1980s throwback era of home-made, shiny ball gowns with long, full skirts and puffy sleeves. Most of us had no experience of going out with boys or girls, and it was a profoundly awkward event for anyone outside the central cool and beginning-to-be-sexually-experienced group. Being put on display was awful when you did not yet feel right in your skin. The teachers, of course, just wanted to put on a lovely event for us, but it was hard.

Natasha liked sixth form and was elected our head girl.

'I just felt very relaxed, and whether it pushed me enough… I mean, there was zero careers advice – it was all reliant on what you were getting from home. But maybe that was just education in the 1980s and '90s. There was no social media, thank goodness.'

Natasha's immediate peer group centred on the village Baptist church, which insulated her from some of the pressures around teen sex.

'It was quite straightforward. Sex wasn't on the agenda; snogging boys was and that was fun. Talking about boys was of course. It would not be until my twenties that that got questioned. I had a little boyfriend in the church youth group when I was about fourteen, and I didn't even kiss him, because I was too scared to kiss him. Well, not too scared, I just didn't…'

Natasha, like all of us, can't remember any sex education at school.

'I mean, we must have done something. If we did anything, we would have done it in a science lesson. Science was badly taught at Highfield. Really badly taught. Somewhere in the mix of it, there might've been a lesson where we were taught the biology of it. I don't remember talking about it anywhere else!'

Natasha's mum, being the practical and open sort of woman she was, helped a bit.

'She sat down and drew me drawings because she knew all the anatomy! It was another biology lesson! And then she would slip things into conversation all the time like, "Well, if you get really drunk, that often leads to people getting pregnant." So I used to think, *Right, I mustn't get really drunk then*. And she just made remarks like that, and it made me really uncomfortable.'

Natasha's mother was by this time a specialist in child and adolescent psychiatry who worked extensively with troubled youth, including underage teenage mothers. I suspect she was not too worried about the prospect of her daughter falling pregnant accidentally. Perhaps she just wanted to make sure the lines of communication were open, and this was the best way she knew how.

We talk about the fact that both our mothers were – are – feminists, but that, although they came of age in the 1960s, they weren't exactly hippies or participants in the counterculture either. Certainly, they didn't (at least, not to our knowledge!) join in with the sexual liberation of their generation. But they must have been influenced by it, as all cultures filter down, even to more conservative groups, so we wonder why they found it difficult to talk to us about it all.

Natasha asks, 'I mean, even today, does your mum talk about sex?'

No, she doesn't.

'I can talk to my mum about anything, but I don't talk to her about my sex life. Why don't I talk to her about it?'

To me, it does not seem the most obvious thing to talk to your mother about. You might talk to her about parenting, mothering, work, friendships, relationships. But your sex life? That seems to me a limited avenue of conversation.

It doesn't occur to Natasha either: 'My mum was present at the birth of both my babies, so she's been really involved. I just would never talk to her about *that!*'

There was no information from school, and only vague warnings or instructions from parents. And the message from church was: no sex before marriage. This seems quite quaint now, and I wonder if churches still teach this, or if they've come up to date as some of them have in other areas of human sexuality.

'It was black and white, and then it got layered over with plenty of guilt, and it lines you up to expect to be married at twenty, twenty-one. And the problem you've got to deal with is, "What if I'm not married at twenty-one?" Which is what I had to deal with in my twenties.

After leaving school, Natasha and I were both going to university to study languages, so we decided to go to France for six months to work as au pairs in Bordeaux. We lived in different parts of the region, though close enough that we still socialized in the city. The other au pairs we met came from all over Europe, including a fair number of privately educated (but quite rebellious) girls from the UK who were unleashed on the young men of south-western France.

Natasha recalls, 'That was when I met promiscuous girls. Up till then, I knew it was going on at school, but none of my little friendship group were like that. So yeah, those girls in Bordeaux, that was when I got my reality about what girls of our age do.'

We agreed that we, as a friendship group of girls in sixth form, were quite innocent and inexperienced. And it was not just to do with religion either. We had other friends who didn't go to church but who seemed to have a similarly restrained moral compass.

Meeting a different type of girl was, along with living in France, a bit of a culture shock – it seemed to be all or nothing.

'That's the bit I was really shocked at, just meeting people who would just go for it, anywhere with anyone. And I just remember thinking, do they not have any sense of… this is a precious thing!'

Natasha also spent a year living in Belgium as part of her university degree in European Studies. I ask her how it has affected her outlook, having two years living abroad in francophone countries.

'I think it's really impacted me. I was devastated by Brexit… I couldn't believe how strongly I felt about it because I just love being European! I just think, why on earth have we distanced ourselves from it? I just love all the opportunity it gave us. Language opens up culture and understanding of people. And I love the fact that, when we skipped off to France when we were eighteen, I remember writing letters that said, "I'm not that far away, but life is so different here! And they think so differently!" And just being acutely aware that language opened that understanding, because you could sit – and our French wasn't great – and you could listen and understand. We followed a lot of French by then, and we picked up a lot. And then the year in Brussels was very much pan-European, so I would meet people from every corner of Europe.'

Natasha and I were quite pleased with ourselves that we could speak another language. But then, as Natasha reminds me, 'You'd turn around and meet an eighteen-year-old who spoke French, German, you know, and they were Danish, so they had five languages, all of them pretty good, and you just think, *Oh, my gosh*! But I felt genuinely proud to be part of this wider culture. I felt so passionate about our history and identity here, and so grateful for those opportunities.'

For Natasha, her twenties were difficult years.

'It was the first time in my life that I didn't have a direction, so everything had been laid out until the end of university, and then there was, "What am I going to do for a job? No idea." Again, this was where my mother's impact was a bit of a pain, because she used to say, "Well, I always knew from the age of fourteen I wanted to be a doctor!"'

But Natasha didn't know what she wanted to do. Her father encouraged her to go into the public sector, because of the job security, but there wasn't anything that appealed to her. In the end, Natasha joined a logistics company.

'I just applied for graduate training schemes, and this was one of them, and I found myself in Trafford Park, Manchester, like a fish out of water! I must have been this posh southerner surrounded by proper Mancunians… I just didn't know what I was doing… thinking, *What am I doing? I just don't know what to do with my life.* I don't remember it being particularly easy.'

Natasha felt lost, and this feeling was compounded by the example she had from her mother, a successful and driven career woman who'd settled down and married young.

'I didn't know what to do or who I was at this point. I had so little confidence in what I had to offer, and that was the big difference between us and private-school children. The girls we met. Private-school girls just had this confidence that what they could offer was… fantastic, who they were was fantastic. I didn't have that at all! I used to go to work thinking, *Why am I here? Why are they paying me? I'm a fraud! I don't deserve to be getting my payslip at the end of the month*! And that didn't leave me until my mid-thirties, I don't think. So that is a problem. I think school didn't give me the confidence in who I was as a person, and what I can do.'

Nevertheless, Natasha went on to have a successful and well-paid career in logistics and the charity sector, and she continued in full-time work until her eldest child was almost five, at which point she took a part-time job more locally.

Natasha has followed in her mother's footsteps in having two children, a daughter then a son, and living in the same village. She met her husband, Ben, online in the very early days of internet dating, around 2006, 2007.

'This was in the days before the Tinders… Those days, when you used to do internet dating, it was quite a slow burner. You'd email them and they'd email back a couple of days later, and then you'd email again. And in the end, after about a month, he said, "Shall we talk on the phone?"'

Natasha and Ben finally met when he came for a job interview at the charity where she worked.

'We sat in the staffroom and had a coffee and a chat, and then I remember going back to my desk, and saying to some girl, "He's lovely!" because I had dated some duffers. And that was that really!'

She met him after his interview and says the rest is history: 'I was head over heels, straight away, and he was the same! It was so straightforward.'

It had not been straightforward for Natasha though, being brought up (intentionally or not) with the expectation she would just meet a man in her early twenties and get married soon afterwards. She met and married Ben when she was thirty, thirty-one, which now doesn't seem very late.

'Now you look at it and think, *What was I worried about?*'

But at the time she felt like she'd been left on the shelf. She had her daughter, her first child, at thirty-four. Her mother supported her through the births, and she found the baby stage straightforward.

'They both latched on, and they fed from day one, and I lost weight – I'm just naturally built to be a feeding machine! In three weeks, I was back in my jeans, and I was quite bored. Because with Isabella, you just fed her, put her down, and thought, *What do I do now?* I signed up for a study about eating allergies or something. They needed breastfed babies. We did things like that, and I went to baby groups.'

Natasha found it all very easy compared to other mothers, to the point that she considered it quite dull.

I ask her about how she felt about breastfeeding, given this is something that is very much promoted in the UK now. Uptake among certain demographics is high and much lower in others.

'I felt fine about it. Absolutely fine. I'm not embarrassed of breastfeeding. My mother-in-law was the only one who would go on about the bottle, but I just thought, *Oh, whatever.* My mum was a much stronger factor in that for me than my mother-in-law.'

Because Natasha's mother had breastfed, that was a choice that came naturally to her.

'But I do remember, especially with Joseph, oh my gosh I was ready to stop. I did enough – I think at eleven months I got him off the boob. Isabella was more like fifteen months. And then I had a friend around the same time who was going for a couple of years, and I just thought, *Ugh, how can you keep going?* I just didn't get it at that point.'

Breastfeeding (or not) is a very personal decision for each mother at that stage, when the baby is past a year old. I was also very dedicated to breastfeeding my children, and carried on until they were past eighteen months, but by then I had definitely had enough. As soon as I'd stopped, I felt a little repulsed by other people doing it, which took me by surprise as I had enjoyed it myself.

Natasha understands this change of feeling.

'I feel sorry for people who can't breastfeed, then they're pumping [expressing their breast milk], and I just think, *For goodness' sake, bottle! Why do you bother?* But obviously I hold myself back from saying that. But I just think, *What are you putting yourself through?* I expressed for ages. I had to go on a course, because I was going back to work. I expressed all this milk, and they didn't touch a drop of it!'

We laugh about what now seem such comedic efforts to lovingly express our milk, with machines, like Friesian cows, and at how it was all wasted because our babies just wouldn't ever take a bottle. These are things you can't ever understand until you have a baby with a will of its own.

'You know, the other day, I met this lady in the village who really wanted to be my friend, and I just don't… she's had a baby, and I'm just not interested in going around and talking about it. I don't want to hold the newborn! I'm just not interested! So it was all fine, it was lovely, but I'm glad I was older and had more going on in my life. If that had been it, at twenty-three, where I had zero career and thought this was going to make me… I mean, what a joke. Being a mum is not going to make you. It just becomes a part of you, but it's not *all* of you. I don't believe that.'

Overall, Natasha appreciates her children a lot more now they have become more defined human beings.

'Now it's fabulous! I don't think I'm very maternal. I love them much more now! I'm so happy to be out of the baby years. Fourteen to twenty months – oh my gosh, it's awful! They just scream, they can't particularly talk, they cry all the time. And my two are early risers, so I had, for ages, 4.30, 5 o'clock starts. And I look at the pictures now and think, *Oh, you were really cute.* But the reality was it was just hard work. Relentless, relentless, relentless. And now they're just these lovely people, and they're so fun and enjoyable. I think you just have to endure the baby years. I'm just glad I didn't do it any earlier in my life because I think I'd have just been made miserable by it! I love being a mum, but… being a mum, to me, doesn't equate to having a baby. It's the other stuff.'

Natasha adds, 'That's what makes me think, about people who adopt and foster… I just find it incredible because I just can't quite imagine having that amount of love and patience. Because I can have compassion for a child that's needy, but to have that twenty-four-seven? I can give it to grown-ups, I can give something of myself to people that are rational.'

I ask Natasha how she envisages things will be for her daughter growing up.

'I think the pressure… the academic achievement will be much harder on her. I think the state system is now… about striving, you strive. We were never pushed to think we've got to attain this highly, but we did what we could, and we were praised for it. We were nurtured. What's going to come a lot earlier for our children is that push, and that ambition, and that comparison.'

Natasha says at one local junior school the children seem to be streamed even for sport, and the kids are aware whether they are in the A or the B stream. She tells me about a young girl who she met recently.

'She just made this comment, "We have to strive to be in the best sets, because that's what we have to do."'

Natasha feels it's madness that girls are made to feel they must push themselves in this way.

'This is like a microcosm of the world that Isabella is stepping into, of where she's going. And I know she'll do it, because she's bright, but she's going to spend her whole teen years striving... and then it's going to be about trying to show her that her whole worth doesn't come from all that. It comes from who she is as a person.'

Natasha also thinks social media is already a major challenge.

'Oh my gosh, I have no idea how to cope. This... it's one of my big things, is TV and controlling what they watch, and walking in when they're watching these stupid things. ... It's all so crappily gendered, so the boys' stuff is all Lego, and there's this stupid girls' cartoon, which has these girls with these big eyes and skinny waists. And the dynamic between the girls, even though they're only fourteen, supposedly. I'm thinking, *Oh, this is her model of what girls are like*? It's just so crap, but I'm not coping very well with that bit at the moment.'

My own daughter, who is ten like Natasha's daughter, counts among her 'favourite YouTubers' a plastic-ish, heavily made-up, cutesy, cartoonish young woman (apparently) called Gloom. It all seems so vacuous, but I figure that as long as their time online is a bit limited, there is only so much it can influence them. Harry Potter, and all the spin-off stuff, is, mercifully, still a much stronger presence in her life.

I do wonder, given that both Natasha's daughter and mine are being raised by mothers who have only a very limited interest in make-up, hair styling and fashion, and who studied at university and have had professional careers, the extent to which their dominant role models will be us, and the extent to which they will be these virtual people with pouty lips and swooshing eyelashes.

There are, of course, positive role models in the popular media – Billie Eilish, Lorde and Taylor Swift are among the more interesting and creative public personas that my daughter aspires to. I tell Natasha that my husband has told our children that they're not allowed smartphones until they're sixteen, and they accept it – for the moment, at least.

Natasha pauses. 'We'll never get away with that around here. They have those sorts of things in Year 6 around here. I'm not saying she has to…'

Natasha would like to be able to hold out until the children are fourteen, but the pressures are immense.

'At Christmas, we saw her cousins, so they're fourteen and eleven, and they play with my two for a couple of hours. But a few hours in, they're both sat on their phones, so the model that my children are being presented with is that once you're eleven, twelve, thirteen, you're on a phone.'

This feels hard to resist, for Natasha.

'I have no idea how to cope with it, but I realize that so much of it is about values and self-esteem and spending time with them.

'The stuff I'm really proud of is that my kids have a tolerance in their culture. They're not going to grapple with "Is homosexuality right or wrong?" They're just going to accept people as they are. They're not going to grapple with different religions. They're just accepting of religion and its value and worth.'

Finally, I ask Natasha how she feels about turning forty.

'I like it! I like being in my forties. I feel like… I've done the babies. I've done a bit of career. I've moved away from pursuing a career at the moment, so I feel quite free from that, because when you're in it, the career thing, you think that's the be all and end all, but actually, when you step away from it, you think… so what? I'm exploring different things. I'm going to be the paper candidate in the local elections for the Lib Dem party!'

Natasha's local constituency is strongly Conservative, like most of the Home Counties, and it has only ever had a Lib Dem councillor once in the last forty years. We laugh about the fact that she doesn't actually want to win – she just wants to be involved, to contribute to the conversation. Perhaps one reason I gravitated towards the people I did at school (like Natasha) was because they were among the few people whose parents shared the morals and politics of my parents – anti-Thatcher essentially. Sort of left of centre but essentially liberal, although socially conservative on certain issues.

Natasha feels that now is an expansive time of life.

'I just like meeting the different people I'm getting to meet. It's quite a unique time in life, I feel. I've got a bit of school, a bit of community life. My parents are healthy; all our parents are healthy. They're actively involved with the kids. My sister-in-law says this a lot, she says we'll look back and these will be the golden years. We'll look back at when our children were happy to be with us, enjoyed us, and our company! I think this is as good as life gets really.'

I suggest to Natasha that she's a real optimist, and she agrees: 'I'm very content. But I didn't feel content.'

Still moving in church circles, Natasha says there is pressure and a bit of guilt around at times.

'Faith becomes about giving away your money, the fact that I'm middle class, the fact I've got money, I've got a house.'

Natasha has sometimes felt spiritual guilt about this, but she is trying self-acceptance.

'It's me, it's who I am. Okay, yes. We've got money, we've got a house, and I didn't deserve any of it, you know? My mum and dad gave us a load of money.'

I say to Natasha that, unless you're a super-high earner, most people – I'm talking about professional people on modest and even comfortable salaries – who own houses, in our generation, are those who have been given at least some money by their parents or grandparents.

The funny thing is that, comparatively speaking, Natasha is not especially wealthy (by the standards of the area in which she lives). She tells me they, like me, still receive child benefit payments, which are means tested to ensure they are only received by families below a certain income. Natasha was drawn to a competitive career by her education, the example of her mother, and other motivating factors. But, having tried it, she feels that she has done it, and she sees the benefits, but she sees the drawbacks. She also appreciates the value of time – time that her children and her family need her to devote to them. If she doesn't give them her time, then no one else will, and children do need to be raised.

But I sense that she feels the comparison with local people who are much wealthier.

'But I'm letting go of that. The good thing is that I was earning so much when I worked in my career, but I was able to take a huge pay cut to do this local charity job. And it's good for us as a family, and it's good for my time with the kids. What do I need? What do I need all that money for? I just feel I can be more content with who I am.'

Epilogue

As I reflect on the writing of these chapters and the stories they tell, I am reminded of how quickly time moves on. We are now in our mid-forties, and turning forty is a little further away in years today than turning fifty will be. So what has changed since our mothers were young, and what will be different for our daughters?

As Emma's story has shown, there has been a major cultural shift in how death, loss, and grief are managed for children losing parents, and mothers losing children. Alex and Laura's family story also illustrates how long and complex the journey of loss can be, and how life was dramatically different for women having children in the 1970s and '80s.

The women I interviewed all think that secondary schooling has improved since we were in compulsory education but that the social and academic pressures on children have increased. Our daughters' generation do not necessarily have the resilience of previous generations in handling these pressures. Educationally, the pendulum seems to be swinging away from the freestyle schooling we received in the 1990s towards a more structured provision.

One issue that has landed very firmly on the public agenda during the time I've been writing this book is the feminist controversy over sex and gender identity, and the various possible meanings of the word 'woman'. When I started talking to the women who feature in this book, in 2017–18, it really was not

an obvious topic of conversation. Many women of our generation were educated to perceive 'gender' as something restrictive,
based on rigid cultural and social stereotypes, that therefore
needs dismantling. The second-wave feminists that many of us
read – Simone de Beauvoir, Betty Friedan, and Germaine Greer
– told us that gender is a social construct which has no material
existence.[85] Gender is femininity, and it is not real. The body
is, however, a material reality, to a great extent immutable, that
deeply marks our sexual and social existence, through the effects
of endogenous female sex hormones and the physical processes
of menstruation, pregnancy, childbirth and breastfeeding, and
menopause.

These questions are emerging as the source of a generational
break between women of this generation and our daughters.
Many younger women today, those who have not yet had
children, adopt the view of liberal and postmodern feminism,
namely that womanhood is a question of identity and self-defi-
nition, rather than arising from the material reality of sexed bodies; it is too early to tell how this debate will evolve, although it
is evolving very quickly.[86] Our daughters are part of a generation
that often approaches sex, gender, and gender non-conformity
in a different way, and they will have to find their own way in
that world. They are arguably growing up in a *more* gendered
world than we did – a point convincingly made by the 'Pink
Stinks' campaign of the 2010s, which highlighted the gendered
nature of toys and clothing today compared to the more uni-
sex equivalents of our 1970s and '80s childhoods.[87] But young
women today also exist increasingly in the disembodied, virtual
world of the digital age. We are living through a new crisis of
femininity that might just be, as some feminists have recently
argued, the unintended consequence of the sexual revolution
and mid-twentieth-century countercultures, together with the
new digital technologies.[88]

My interviewees all agreed that we were taught in a low-key
way that we could, as girls, do whatever we wanted. Alison is a
good example – her dream to be a mechanic was unusual for a
girl, but nobody seemed to care when we were at school, and

people accepted her slight 'difference' without question. She has spoken in a nuanced way here about how she both does and does not feel feminine. This has always been a complex question for women, but it is one that tends to find resolution as we age. Alex, too, is highly gender nonconforming, but she has never seriously questioned her femaleness, even though her embodied experience is complex, and she empathises strongly with gender-questioning children today.

The women whose lives are documented here have clearly asserted that they gain happiness and satisfaction from things feminism has sometimes rejected as limiting – marriage, family, babies. 'The housewife's life is not real,' Germaine Greer told us, in her 1970 classic, *The Female Eunuch*: 'The refusal to accept this as a rewarding life is not a refusal to accept reality.'[89] I do not think that many women with children would agree with this view today. Greer has never been a housewife, and her perfectly rational choice *not* to have children cannot easily be projected onto other women. She was also writing in a different era, and the life of the 1970s suburban housewife could be isolating and limiting – although I do not think it was so for my own mother, who gained intellectual stimulation from all the voluntary organizational work she did and the lively social connections it generated.

Nevertheless, what these conversations have also revealed is that it is difficult – if not impossible – to generalize about women's experiences of motherhood. Although many women say they find great fulfilment in raising children, motherhood is also a source of ambivalence, and elements of the role can be difficult and limiting. This adds weight to arguments made by feminists who have critiqued the deterministic idea of a universal maternal instinct that guides our choices and reifies the mother–child bond. As Alex's, Alison's, and Natasha's stories have shown, a woman's relationship to her own body and to her child (or the one she cares for) is not always straightforward. Caring can be 'relentless'; breastfeeding can be stressful, dysphoria-inducing, and downright alienating; children's demands for affection can be suffocating. If we are honest with ourselves, it is this way for all of us at times.

Equally, women often express ambivalence about careers that confer status but which take them away from their children – at least when they are very young. They want equality, and they desire a certain level of intellectual or professional fulfilment, but they do not necessarily crave the public recognition that men seem to seek out, and they are uncomfortable with the idea of farming out childcare to other people. We seem to agree in our conversations that children must be raised properly, that they need to be rooted in communities; many elements of local communities have historically been galvanized by women.

In the absence of the structural changes necessary to enable mothers *and* fathers to work part-time in careers and raise small children at the same time, many women actively choose acceptance of a home-based role; but many women, like Anna, find it exasperating that women's careers are still being limited in this way. Increasingly, as in my own case, men are stepping up and stepping into the role of primary parent, at least after the early years. Indeed, many men find the world of 'work' and 'career' as perplexing as women; there just has not until recently been an obvious alternative. This is something that has changed greatly since we were children, although, as Natasha's story has shown, men were beginning in the 1980s to share domestic and childcare responsibilities in a way unknown in their parents' generation.

As Mary Ingham noted in the 1980s, 'The conflict between a woman's child-rearing capacity and her capability of earning her own living stems from the way in which industrialized society separates work from home.'[90] This question has been revisited by contemporary feminist thinkers who have reasserted the intensity of the symbiotic, physical attachment between women and their children. Most mothers want to work, but they often don't want to work full-time, and their clear preference is – where possible – to take a longish period of maternity leave when their children are babies.[91]

Mary Ingham realized this when she was contemplating the same dilemmas for women of thirty a generation ago. Virginia Novarra echoed Greer's sentiment when she nonsensically complained, in

1980, that years of child-rearing 'can result in a woman's needing a refresher course in being a mentally active human being'. To which Mary Ingham responded, 'Somehow I cannot believe Ms Novarra has any children of her own.'[92] Mary noted, towards the end of her book on turning thirty, that some of the women she'd interviewed 'found that thirty marked the point at which they reached the third phase of their lives, when the large part of their mothering role was accomplished and they could turn to themselves'.[93] At forty-five, we are only just beginning to finish with this mothering role.

Many women prove themselves academically and in careers but later realize that they do not want to have to choose between doing a job and being present as a mother. This is a real dilemma for many women, and I have many talented friends and colleagues who have given up careers that they might have continued had it been possible to work part-time. The workplace is still structured, with a few exceptions, as though all jobs are being done by 1970s men working nine to five, home in time for dinner at 6–7 p.m. The Covid-19 pandemic of 2020–21 of course has changed this, and it is too early to tell what the long-term benefits and drawbacks of this structural shift will be.

The existence of 'imposter syndrome' perhaps shows that many women unfortunately still feel that they go about their professional lives as imposters in a masculine realm. For lots of us, life is better at forty than it's ever been, but it also follows a period of gradual realization that we cannot have everything we desire in life. In private conversations with some of my female academic colleagues who are also mothers, the acceptance of slow career progress, or of having made only a small (but respected) contribution to a field, is a theme. Nevertheless, I am hopeful that as the period of early child-rearing comes definitively to a close for us, we will be able to re-engage with our careers and find renewed satisfaction in pushing forward with new research plans and creative projects.

Kate and Alison found that having children has given their lives meaning and purpose, even though they had already proved themselves to be capable in the workplace. Some of Mary Ingham's interviewees in the late 1970s felt the same way.

One of them, Sylvia, observed: 'I quite enjoyed going out to work, but I'm happiest in the times spent as a family. I've been surprised at the satisfaction I've got from having children, taking them places or the little chats we have, simple things like making things for them and seeing my daughter's face light up when she sees me. I can't see working at a career would satisfy me as much, but you don't know, do you, when you're young?'[94]

As I was completing this book, I got back in touch with all the women to whom I'd spoken and whose stories feature here. I want to end with their words to give an impression of life now, as we settle into our forties. The pandemic has touched all our lives, and has had the positive effect of allowing women and men to work more flexibly and closer to home. Women have, of course, taken more responsibility at home for looking after children during lockdown and seeing to their schooling online.[95] Time will tell what the impact will be.

One effect of the pandemic has been to reverse the geographical separation of home life and working life which had otherwise grown undisturbed since the Industrial Revolution, and I think that home working is here to stay. This is convenient for those who had to commute several times a week, but the mode of home working is more isolated and isolating. A chat on screen is no substitute for sitting down with another person and catching up over a coffee during a break at work. Women and men have surely reacted differently to this shift. As we all know, for Boris Johnson the distraction is the fridge full of cheese. For women, I wonder, is it the pile of dirty washing-up or the floor that needs endlessly to be hoovered when there are kids in the house?

Anna continues to work in the same job in the charity sector and has had to adapt quickly to new working patterns, as well as to new parenting challenges.

'Since giving this interview it seems like the world has turned upside down with the pandemic, and the resulting blurring of family and work life all centred at home for us. This has both advantages and disadvantages; I miss being out and about in the office and desperately miss the travel my work normally entails, although I feel fortunate to have kept my job and our family financial security during Covid, and to have got to know my children better. My son is also now diagnosed with ADHD and ASD and receiving enhanced support at school which has been an adjustment. The pandemic has put huge pressure on everyone – but I do worry about women and girls especially in the developing world, where the absences of school and childcare have placed enormous pressure on women's working lives.'

Kate's daughters are now grown up and some of them are settled and have enjoyed educational successes. It seems likely that she will be a grandmother soon. Although it was difficult for Kate becoming a young, unmarried mother at nineteen, single motherhood no longer carries the shame and stigma that it did in our mothers' generation, when teenagers who fell pregnant were virtually compelled to give up their babies for adoption. Kate wishes she had made more of some of the opportunities she had earlier in her life but has no regrets about the family she has raised.

Emily's life continues to be stable and her career successful, although she says she would take back her remarks about our daughters' generation eschewing social media!

'When I reflect on my story from 2017, a few things stand out,' she says. 'Comparing my education to the one my children received, I would now say my education could have been better. On social media, my children do not use Facebook, but they do spend time on other social platforms. I do believe social media has caused additional anxiety for my children and other teenagers and that the idea of social-media feeds being constantly viewed and rated is inherently bad for them.

'In the shadow of the climate crisis, the owning of three cars now feels pretty scandalous, though at the time it was necessary to get the children to school and each of us to work. I'm not sure how this will improve without real social change and better transport infrastructure – and there doesn't seem to be real focus for change from the government on this. I'm not sure how some of these large social issues will be resolved. As a species we seem to struggle to collaborate on large issues internationally, and as individuals we feel powerless to act. It can all feel a little hopeless, so people take a head-in-the-sand approach…'

Emma continues to excel professionally. She has found healing and a significant measure of self-acceptance, and has been able finally to establish an amicable relationship with her daughter's father.

'I passed my MSc to be a nurse practitioner with merit; I have been qualified for three years now. It is my dream job and I love it. During the height of the pandemic, I was one of twenty-two clinical leads for NHS Test and Trace which I am incredibly proud about. I left to give myself some work–life balance once lockdown was lifted, which is something I have never had before. … Lockdown forced me to have some intensive therapy as I could no longer run away from my issues. This has been the best thing I've ever done for myself.

'I have now cut all ties with my family with no regrets. Milly is now twenty; she moved to Manchester two years ago to live with a guy she met working in Greece. He is a lovely lad, a policeman. She has passed her driving test and is now a duty manager in a pub, a job she loves. Despite the distance, we are still close and get on better now than when she lived at home. On her twentieth birthday we went for a meal, and she invited her dad too, which he was over the moon about. I have a campervan and have spent this year travelling around the UK. Next year I plan to drive around Europe. My house is sold so I am currently on the hunt for a barn conversion in the countryside… and those chickens!'

Alex and **Laura** continue to be outstanding in their careers. Alex is actively looking for a primary-school headship, and Laura is likely to be promoted to full professor soon. On the home front, Alex is still a crucial support to Laura in bringing up her two adopted daughters. Now Laura's eldest child has hit adolescence, life has become challenging, and secondary school is compounding many of her emotional issues. Laura is currently looking into trying to secure alternative provision for her that will help to meet her needs. Both the girls attended school throughout the pandemic as they needed the institutional stability to function, and, for Laura, it made working from home possible as a single mother.

Alison's family life continues to flourish. She is finding her feet back in the world of work and is enjoying getting her hands dirty again. The dog idea didn't work out for them in the end.

'We only had him for a week before I returned him to the breeders. It makes me sound like the worst person in the world, but I couldn't bear putting him in his crate every night and listening to him cry. He never stopped all night, even after five days. I don't regret it and think it was the right decision at the time. We now have a cat…

'I've changed my job too. I still work for the same school but in the technology department as their technician. I really love it. I prepare all the wood and metal the students need for the lessons, and look after all the machines in the department. I sometimes support in lessons too. I've learnt how to weld and get to use table saws, lathes, and other machines most days. It's term time too so I still get to be home with my son in the holidays. Lockdown was a challenge, like it was for most people, I think. I spent most of it home-schooling and in the garden. Lockdown wasn't the easiest time where work was concerned, but there were a lot more people who had a harder time than us.'

Kim is enjoying her young daughter's toddler years and is faced with new challenges now as a stay-at-home mum who has put her career on hold.

'It is now November 2021, and due to the Covid-19 pandemic, my world has continued to remain small. I previously spoke of living in a bubble of my immediate family and those close to me. That seems not to have changed significantly. My daughter is now three, and she has only just begun a few mornings a week at nursery this term, and until then has been 100 per cent of the time with me. We have had minimal childcare support – heightened due to Covid lockdowns, etc. – so it has been intense. Yet I think that of all the times in mine and Mia's life it could have happened, this period has afforded the least disruption to her and us. She has mainly wanted my attention and this period provided that – fully!

'As we begin exploring schools for her, I'm having to face my own disillusionment with the education system and am trying to discern what will support her best, which is personally quite challenging. I'm also getting closer to wanting to re-engage with my own career path. In the current climate of 60 per cent of midwives wanting to leave the profession due to stress and poor working conditions, I think my skills and experience might serve best in supporting mothers, NHS workers, and others rather than trying to dip in or dive back into a profession I left for the same reasons. There is a lot still unknown, but as I get a little more time in the coming months to give consideration to life beyond motherhood, I look forward to responding to what emerges. It has been an intense and challenging time, but again one I feel immense gratitude for given all that has been provided for me personally.'

Natasha still enjoys living in the village and likes having slightly older children. She continues to be enthusiastically involved in the life of her local area.

'Needless to say, I didn't win the local election; I decided I wasn't motivated enough by local politics after all. I had an amazing time during lockdown with the kids. I got to know them really well, learnt to follow their passions, and spent lots of time outdoors exploring together. It was all good, and although during those giddy, self-directed learning days I did consider home-schooling, I recognized I wasn't cut out for it in the long term, so when they went back to school in September 2020, I got a new job.

'I now work for a large organization delivering safeguarding training, which has been interesting. I feel I'm getting my career going again and can see lots of potential ways it might develop. My parents are starting to age – Dad especially. Mum is still a whirlwind (although her energy levels are now more limited) and has set up a charity over the past couple of years serving the elderly in our village. I have finally stopped comparing myself to her and now see the value in my own path. Yippee! All in all, this whole experience has been very interesting and felt quite self-indulgent, so thank you for wading through all those transcribed pages of my drunken waffle and so many congratulations for making sense of it all.'

Afterword

BY MARY INGHAM

It has been a pleasure to be a small part of the process where-by Susannah Wilson's idea became a concrete project she has realized in book form. Achieving this alongside balancing a demanding career with her family life and responsibilities earns my greatest admiration.

My book *Now We Are Thirty*, based on interviews with others of my year at school, was prefaced with the quote Susannah has also used, from an A.A. Milne poem about Milne's son Christopher, aged six, walking hand in hand with his best friend, Anne, sharing their dreams of what they would be doing when they were forty-two. *Now We Are Thirty* was a sort of way station towards that stage of adult life, a snapshot of women I was at school with, at thirty. Susannah has fulfilled the full promise of Milne's poetic image by interviewing a selection of her own classmates at the age of forty.

As Susannah points out, a book, like a child, develops a life of its own. In idea form, her study mirrored mine, in terms of wanting to know what other women from her year at school have made of their lives. But *Now We Are Forty* inevitably grew and formed a different shape from *Now We Are Thirty*. It is more close-focused, concentrating in depth on a small group of women from Susannah's year at school. As such, *Now We Are Forty* explores more personal detail of individual backgrounds, lifestyle choices, motives, experiences, opinions, and concerns than my own study.

How do Susannah's classmates' lives compare with those of the women I interviewed at thirty – effectively their mothers' generation? Our education was different: single-sex grammar school rather than mixed comprehensive; the economic climate then was very different; the state of play in terms of sex roles, expectations, and opportunities for women has certainly changed. Some aspects have developed positively and eased, although new pressures now exist – including whether to use Botox – and concerns about social-media influences on their daughters.

It has interested me to read a little about my peers, Susannah's interviewees' mothers' lives, and learn whether they had ambition for their daughters. The main focus and interest, however, are her classmates themselves: their experience of school, careers advice, and the working world; how they handled motherhood and the family unit; the interplay between their work and home persona; and hopes for their own daughters.

Very noticeable to me is the greater freedom of choice this group of women express in their lives, their more confident and effective agency. Motherhood forms a large and significant part, but so does their own personal fulfilment, and their own working life. They seem better able either to view themselves as navigating different phases of life, each with its own sense of fulfilment, or else to negotiate combining motherhood and work. Their choice not always involves the help and support of a partner – and in the case of pursuing a dual work/home role is not without stress and some discontent.

The 1996 Employment Rights Act and 1999 Maternity and Parental Leave etc. Regulations formed a step in the right direction, in protecting jobs while allowing for time out around the birth, but having a child is still treated like a temporary incapacity, rather than a long-term commitment to raising a future member of society. Some progress has been made in terms of balancing career and motherhood roles, but there remains clearly much more to be done: in some respects, in terms of more accessible childcare; in others, changing societal values – promoting the opportunity to take time out from a career to raise one's own children, rather than having to abide by male-work-oriented schedules, and farm them out to strangers.

In the meantime, after being fired two days after telling her boss she was pregnant, another member of Susannah's generation (and, by implication, one of my generation's daughters), Joeli Brearley officially launched, in 2016, the very vocal campaign group 'Pregnant Then Screwed', drawing attention to the pressures on women becoming mothers, including insufficient affordable childcare and the fact that the current work structure simply does not work for women.

Noticeably, the only childless woman interviewed is childless by choice; and even she is helping raise her twin sister's child. This seems to reflect greater confidence (with more effective fertility treatment, and opportunities for adoption) in postponing pregnancy, as well as less pressure to be part of a conventional nuclear family, with more freedom of choice.

For Susannah's interviewees, parenthood did not necessarily mean marriage first, as it did for my own generation. Kate has clearly helped pioneer single parenthood. And twin sisters Alex and Laura have successfully created an alternative to the nuclear family. The women Susannah has interviewed have tended to marry later, not feel obliged, socially or emotionally, to marry before the birth of their first child, as my own generation did, and may not marry at all. Kate, the single mother, values the fulfilment of motherhood and family above all else but points out that it doesn't define her.

Girls of my generation – and our parents – were encouraged to believe work was simply a temporary hiatus for young women before we married and started a family. A husband would determine our futures, underwrite our financial security. Among Susannah's interviewees, Emily's parents, like mine, had no aspirations for her, didn't consider her future, as Emily does with her own daughter. Emily's experience of the school's low expectations was fortunately counteracted by role models among her peers, other pupils whose aspirations inspired her. Emily carved out her own career after leaving school. She gives her motivation as insecurity, and the need to be financially independent – no assumption that a man would take care of her future.

Judging from these interviews, some aspects appear not to have changed much; and a comprehensive education was in some respects a mixed blessing. One interviewee complains that there was no careers advice. Alison, however, offers a very inspiring example of careers advice, parental support, and personal ambition. Her pioneering career within motor mechanics brings to mind one of my interviewees: Deirdre, an engineering student, one of only two girls among seventy-five students on her university course. Alison's work-experience stint while still at school was with a local garage, encouraged by her father, whom she helped with car maintenance at weekends. (The only work experience scheduled on the timetable at my grammar school was needlework and a term of domestic science, where we learnt basic cookery and how to wash up.) After Alison was blatantly deprived of an apprenticeship on the basis of gender, rather than ability, her father helped her take her case to the Equal Opportunities Commission and make national news by winning it, along with £24,000 compensation.

In the mid-1960s, Deirdre, on the other hand, met with discouragement from the very start. She had been inspired seeing a film at the cinema about girls studying mechanical engineering, and the physics mistress helped her find out more. But, believing she wouldn't survive the course, all the other teachers tried to put her off, telling her she'd 'never make a mechanical engineer'. This made Deirdre furious and stimulated her determination to do it. Fortuitously, when she applied to university 'all the colleges wanted to show they were up with the trend' by having a few token girls on their course.

Deirdre had managed to get a job at the local coal board the summer before the course started. That introduced her right away to male prejudice in the profession, encountering 'rude comments', like, 'You'd better not do that; I'll do it.' It felt wrong to be accepted only once you had proved yourself. 'And of course, the law stated that a woman couldn't work down a mine', which gave the men ammunition to criticize her for being too much 'on the clean side', not knowing what the actual job was like. As a result, she began seriously to question whether she was doing the right thing. Fortunately, her fellow students and the lecturers at Loughborough University treated her as an equal, and finding she was doing as well as the boys reinforced her confidence.

After graduating, Deirdre left behind her 'crowd of college friends' and took a job in Coventry, where she knew no one. She explained that 'it was a matter of making your own life' and deliberately avoided returning to the coal board in her home town. 'It was more important to make a fresh start somewhere I'd be accepted as a professional equal.'

Motherhood has become more accessible for Susannah's generation – in that there are more choices when it comes to fertility treatment or adoption, no pressure to be married, and more time within which to establish one's own path in life before the responsibility of raising a family. Choice of when and whether to have a child was very much created by easy accessibility to the pill. While my own generation had great difficulty obtaining it before marriage, the GP of one of Susannah's interviewees put her on the pill at fifteen. However, the pill prescribed after marriage enabled those of my own generation who married to begin the process of working longer, putting off motherhood until our late twenties and occasionally beyond.

The falling birth rate in the early 1970s triggered governmental concern, when, armed by education and the pill, married women flooded the jobs market and showed no sign of having children. It must surely have been a factor in the maternity leave provisions of the 1975 Employment Protection Act, passed, ironically, shortly before the tide began to turn, as our generation faced the then scary 'elderly primigravida' age of thirty, which began an upward trend leading to the birth of Susannah's generation.

At forty, Susannah's interviewees seem much more self-confident than my peers at thirty. They have more independent, self-assertive lives, with more choices as a result. They seem more rooted, more sure of themselves as women. However, despite the progress they demonstrate, some of the problems and conflicts remain: Anna claims sex education was not properly taught; that they sleepwalked through their career choices. And, despite advances in fertility treatment and adoption, the dilemmas of childcare are still polarizing roles, with a few pioneering exceptions.

The central issue remains fundamentally the same. Anna begs the question – how to combine the realities of career and childcare? Should women emulate men or embrace a different idea of what makes life meaningful? She sees the main issue facing women today being that of combining a family and a career. Women have mostly been the ones who have had to make compromises, abandoned or stepped down in their careers. A few, with the help of their partners, are managing to break that mould. Although – as Susannah herself testifies – it's not easy. The loosening of traditional roles entails women relinquishing some control in the home sphere. Juggling two sets of responsibilities can lead to feeling one is falling short in both. Stepping back may allow a change in direction, rather than accepting working life as a conveyor belt in one direction upwards. And working from home during the pandemic hopefully disrupted a strict work/home divide for both sexes.

The closing page of *Now We Are Thirty* posed a question: must the reality of having children 'dictate so much of our lives that it forces all of us, men and women, into a straitjacket of interdependent, yet strangely separate worlds'? It was a question that at the time I wondered might be solved by the time we were forty-two. Susannah has shown here that, by their lifestyles, relationships, and life choices, at least some of our daughters' generation are feeling their way a little further towards solving it; not least Susannah herself, in researching and producing this book.

Mary Ingham,
Ramsgate, October 2022

Notes

All online sources cited were last accessed on 24 March 2023.

1. Mary Ingham, *Now We Are Thirty* (London: Methuen, 1981).
2. Ibid., 11.
3. Denis Campbell, 'Record numbers of women reach 30 child-free in England and Wales', *The Guardian*, 27 January 2022. In 2020, the standardised mean age of mothers remained unchanged from 2019 at 30.7 years – a record high since data collection began: https://www.ons.gov.uk/peoplepopulationandcommunity/birthsdeathsandmarriages/livebirths/bulletins/birthcharacteristicsinenglandandwales/2020#age-of-parents
4. Ingham, *Now We Are Thirty*, 205.
5. See Mark Chatterton, *Britain's Motorways* (Stroud: Amberley Publishing, 2022).
6. Gareth E. Rees, *Unofficial Britain: Journeys Through Unexpected Places* (London: Elliott & Thompson, 2020), 64.
7. Ingham, *Now We Are Thirty*, 221.
8. See Jacqueline Scott, Shirley Dex and Heather Joshi, *Women and Employment* (Cheltenham: Edward Elgar Publishing, 2008).
9. Derek Gillard, *Education in England* (1987–2022): http://www.educationengland.org.uk/history/chapter15.html
10. Joanne Bailey, 'The History of Mum and Dad: Recent Historical Research on Parenting in England from the

16th to 20th centuries History of British Parenting', *History compass* 12 (6) (June 2014): 489–507.

11. Ingham, *Now We Are Thirty*, 70–71.

12. See chapters by Lesley A. Hall, Ann Blair and Daniel Monk on sex education in 1980s–1990s Britain in Lutz Sauerteig and Roger Davidson (eds), *Shaping Sexual Knowledge: A Cultural History of Sex Education in Twentieth-Century Europe* (London: Routledge, 2009).

13. Katy Greenland, 'The repeal of Section 28', *Pastoral Care in Education* 26 (4) (November 2008): 243–251.

14. See Selina Todd, *The People: The Rise and Fall of the Working Class, 1910–2010* (London: John Murray, 2014) and *Snakes and Ladders: The Great British Social Mobility Myth* (London: Chatto & Windus, 2021).

15. Pat Thane and Tanya Evans, *Sinners? Scroungers? Saints? Unmarried Motherhood in Twentieth-Century England* (Oxford: Oxford University Press, 2012).

16. Kate Proctor, 'PM's single mother remarks "disgusting"', says Angela Rayner', *The Guardian*, 6 December 2019.

17. The ONS recorded 49 per cent of births outside of wedlock in 2021: https://www.ons.gov.uk/peoplepopulationandcommunity/birthsdeathsandmarriages/livebirths/datasets/birthsummarytables

18. Ingham, *Now We Are Thirty*, 86. https://www.gov.uk/government/publications/gcse-results Lesley Andres and Johanna Wyn, *The Making of a Generation: The Children of the 1970s in Adulthood* (Toronto: University of Toronto Press, 2016). Paul Feeney, *Baby Boomer Generation: A Lifetime of Memories* (Stroud: The History Press, 2015).

19. On the history of the GDST, see Janet Sondheimer and P.R. Bodington, *The Girls' Public Day School Trust, 1872–1972: A Centenary Review* (London: Girls' Public Day School Trust, 1972).

20. The UK government notes that 'good performance at GCSE is required if children are to be successful in post-16 education and the labour market'.

https://www.gov.uk/government/publications/
social-mobility-indicators/social-mobility-indicators

21. https://www.gov.uk/government/publications/gcse-results

22. Andres and Wyn, *The Making of a Generation*, 227–228.

23. Feeney, *Baby Boomer Generation*.

24. https://www.ons.gov.uk/peoplepopulationandcommunity/
populationandmigration/internationalmigration/articles/
housingandhomeownershipintheuk/2015-01-22

25. John McCormick, *Contemporary Britain* (Basingstoke:
Palgrave Macmillan, 2012), 71: 'In 1900, just 10 per cent
of Britons owned their own homes, but today the figure is
more than 70 per cent.'

26. Paul Jennings, *A History of Drink and the English,
1500–2000* (London: Routledge, 2016), 86–88.

27. In terms of the class numbering used by the British government, we had few children of parents in category 1, the
higher managerial and professional classes. (McCormick,
Contemporary Britain, 67).

28. McCormick, *Contemporary Britain*, 61.

29. Rebecca Tunstall, *The Fall and Rise of Social Housing: 100
Years on 20 Estates* (Bristol: Policy Press, 2020).

30. McCormick, *Contemporary Britain*, 57.

31. A lifestyle advocated by Lenore Skenazy in *Free-Range Kids:
How to Raise Safe, Self-Reliant Children* (San Francisco:
Jossey-Bass, 2010).

32. A change noted by Greg Lukianoff and Jonathan Haidt in
The Coddling of the American Mind (New York: Penguin,
2018).

33. The 'tomboy' phenomenon in our generation of women is
charted in fascinating detail by Lisa Selin Davis, *Tomboy:
The Surprising History and Future of Girls Who Dare to Be
Different* (New York: Grand Central Publishing, 2021).

34. Michelle Addison, Madeline Breeze and Yvette Taylor
(eds), *The Palgrave Handbook of Imposter Syndrome
in Higher Education* (Cham, Switzerland: Palgrave
Macmillan, 2022).

35. Institute for Fiscal Studies, 'Higher Education Funding in England: Past, Present and Options for the Future' (2017), 2–4: https://ifs.org.uk/uploads/publications/bns/BN211.pdf. See also: Roger Brown and Helen Carasso, *Everything for Sale? the Marketisation of UK Higher Education* (London: Taylor & Francis Group, 2013).

36. Rebecca Asher, *Shattered: Modern Motherhood and the Illusion of Equality* (London: Vintage, 2012), 9.

37. Megan K. Stack, *Women's Work: A Personal Reckoning with Labour, Motherhood, and Privilege* (London: Le Scribe, 2019), x.

38. Ingham, *Now We Are Thirty*, 135.

39. Mary Ingham, *Facing Forty*, (unpublished mamuscript),10.

40. Ingham, *Now We Are Thirty*, 20.

41. Ibid., 49.

42. Ibid., 24.

43. Ibid., 27.

44. Ibid., 53. Referring to the Hadow Report on 'The Education of the Adolescent': http://www.educationengland.org.uk/documents/hadow1926

45. On the Park Fever Hospital, see: https://www.nationalarchives.gov.uk/hospitalrecords/details.asp?id=70. The London Fever Hospital in Islington had 150 beds in 1924, as reported here: 'The London Fever Hospital', *The Spectator*, 12 January 1924, 14. https://archive.spectator.co.uk/article/12th-january-1924/14/the-london-fever-hospital

46. See Geoffrey Rivett, *The History of the NHS* (London: Nuffield Trust, 2019): https://www.nuffieldtrust.org.uk/chapter/inheritance#introduction-the-inheritance-of-the-nhs

47. The average age to marry became steadily lower from the 1950s, for a few decades, until the '70s when couples started marrying later again. See Ingham, *Now We Are Thirty*, 118.

48. Ibid., 28.

49. This scenario is fictionalized in Joanna Trollope's 1991 book, *The Rector's Wife*, in which villagers are scandalized

at the idea of the Anglican rector's wife taking a part-time job in a nearby town.

50. Clive Wilson, *Time of My Life: A Jazz Journey from London to New Orleans* (Jackson: University Press of Mississippi, 2019), 11.

51. A.M. Siegler and A. Grunebaum, 'The 100th anniversary of tubal sterilization', *Fertility and Sterility* 34 (6) (December 1980): 610–613.

52. Ingham, *Now We Are Thirty*, 68.

53. Ibid., 52.

54. https://www.oxford-royale.com/articles/history-womens-education-uk

55. https://www.bbc.co.uk/news/in-pictures-48335039 and https://www.bbc.co.uk/religion/religions/christianity/cofe/cofe_1.shtml#h3

56. The organization's archives begin in 1961: https://discovery.nationalarchives.gov.uk/details/c/F221990 and https://www.eyalliance.org.uk/who-we-are-0

57. Ingham, *Now We Are Thirty*, 47.

58. Ibid., 52.

59. https://www.politics.co.uk/reference/education-leaving-age. On the change to the school leaving age and its impact on youth employment through the 1980s and '90s, when we came of age, see Andy Furlong, John Goodwin, Sarah Hadfield et al., *Young People in the Labour Market: Past, Present, Future* (New York: Routledge, 2017), 1–9.

60. https://rethinkorphanages.org

61. See for example Angela McRobbie's blog post for the London School of Economics on structural inequalities between the sexes: https://blogs.lse.ac.uk/impactofsocialsciences/2015/09/03/womens-working-lives-in-the-managerial-university. Cited in Lisa Downing, *Selfish Women* (Abingdon, Oxon; New York, NY: Routledge, 2019), 118.

62. Ibid., 118–119.

63. Asher, *Shattered*, 6–7.

64. This issue is also addressed by Ingrid Wassenaar in *Motherload: Modern Motherhood and How to Survive It* (London: IPW Books, 2022).
65. https://beerandpub.com/statistics/pub-numbers. According to these statistics, UK pubs declined in numbers from 60,000 to 50,000 in twenty years from 2000–20. The impact of raising tax on beer and of the 2008 financial crisis are also mentioned here: https://www.bbc.co.uk/news/health-40444460
66. Business and Technology Education Council – vocational qualification: https://qualifications.pearson.com/en/about-us/qualification-brands/btec.html
67. McCormick, *Contemporary Britain*, 71.
68. https://www.ons.gov.uk/peoplepopulationandcommunity/personalandhouseholdfinances/incomeandwealth/bulletins/householddisposableincomeandinequality/financialyear2020
69. Ingham, *Now We Are Thirty*, 103.
70. https://www.imdb.com/title/tt0073747
71. According to the *Huffington Post*, which ran a piece on 28 November 2019: 'Boris Johnson Called Children of Single Mothers "Ill-Raised, Ignorant, Aggressive and Illegitimate."' These comments were originally published in *The Spectator* in 1995.
72. See Louise Perry, *The Case Against the Sexual Revolution* (Cambridge: Polity, 2022), 168. On the 'Cinderella effect' Perry cites evolutionary psychologist Steven Pinker, *How the Mind Works* (New York: Norton, 2009), 434.
73. Prenatal screening for Down syndrome developed significantly during the 1990s. See G. Ashoor Al Mahri and K.H. Nicolaides 'Evolution in screening for Down syndrome', *The Obstetrician & Gynaecologist* 21 (1) (October 2018): 51–57.
74. Ingham, *Now We Are Thirty*, 51.
75. This idea was originally conceptualised as 'la charge mentale ' ('the mental load') in French by cartoonist Emma. The cartoon was translated into English in 2017:

'The gender wars of household chores: a feminist comic', *The Guardian*, 26 May 2017.

76. Ingham, *Now We Are Thirty*, 19.

77. https://www.allcourts.co.uk/news/stop-selling-childrens-future-playing-fields

78. https://www.bbc.co.uk/programmes/b0bx7lxc

79. https://www.ox.ac.uk/about/facts-and-figures/admissions-statistics/undergraduate-students/current/school-type

80. https://englishassociation.ac.uk/test-news-post-2 and https://www.museumsassociation.org/museums-journal/news/2021/07/outrage-as-sheffield-university-confirms-closure-of-archaeology-department/#

81. Ingham, *Now We Are Thirty*, 155.

82. This was at a time when the average salary for non-manual females aged between 30 and 39 across the UK was £12,714 (or £244.50 per week): https://www.ons.gov.uk/employmentandlabourmarket/peopleinwork/earningsandworkinghours/adhocs/006810newearningssurveynesagegroupgrossweeklyandhourlyexcludingovertimedata. By comparison, a consultant psychiatrist today in the UK has a starting salary in Year 1 of £84,559: https://www.bma.org.uk/pay-and-contracts/pay/consultants-pay-scales/pay-scales-for-consultants-in-england

83. Ingham, *Now We Are Thirty*, 104.

84. Ibid., 62.

85. Simone de Beauvoir, *Le deuxième sexe* (Paris: Gallimard, 1949); Betty Friedan, *The Feminine Mystique* (Harmondsworth: Penguin, 1965); Germaine Greer, *The Female Eunuch* (London: Flamingo, 1999 [1970]).

86. See for example Laurie Penny, *Sexual Revolution: Modern Fascism and the Feminist Fightback.* (London: Bloomsbury, 2022).

87. 'Campaign against pink toys for girls enjoys rosy outlook', *The Guardian*, 18 December 2011.

88. Perry, *The Case Against the Sexual Revolution* (Cambridge: Polity, 2022).

89. Greer, *The Female Eunuch*, 312.

90. Ingham, *Now We Are Thirty*, 12–13.
91. See Perry, *The Case Against the Sexual Revolution* and Mary Harrington, *Feminism Against Progress* (Corbridge: Forum Books, 2023). https://www.conservativewoman.co.uk/au-contraire-claire-women-want-to-cut-their-work-hours/
92. Ingham, *Now We Are Thirty*, 214–215, citing Virginia Novarra, *Women's Work, Men's Work: The Ambivalence of Equality* (London: Boyars, 1980).
93. Ingham, *Now We Are Thirty*, 211.
94. Ibid., 224.
95. 'Women "put careers on hold" to home-school during UK Covid-19 lockdown', *The Guardian*, 30 July 2020.

Bibliography

Addison, Michelle, Madeline Breeze, and Yvette Taylor (eds).
*The Palgrave Handbook of Imposter Syndrome in Higher
Education* (Cham, Switzerland: Palgrave Macmillan,
2022).

Andres, Lesley and Johanna Wyn. *The Making of a Generation:
The Children of the 1970s in Adulthood* (Toronto:
University of Toronto Press, 2016).

Asher, Rebecca. *Shattered: Modern Motherhood and the Illusion
of Equality* (London: Vintage, 2012).

Ashoor Al Mahri, G. and K.H. Nicolaides. 'Evolution in
screening for Down syndrome', *The Obstetrician &
Gynaecologist* 21 (1) (October 2018): 51–57.

Bailey, Joanne. 'The History of Mum and Dad: Recent
Historical Research on Parenting in England from the
16th to 20th centuries History of British Parenting',
History Compass 12 (6) (June 2014): 489–507.

Beauvoir, Simone de. *Le deuxième sexe* (Paris: Gallimard, 1949).

Brown, Roger and Helen Carasso. *Everything for Sale? The
Marketisation of UK Higher Education* (London: Taylor &
Francis Group, 2013).

Chatterton, Mark. *Britain's Motorways* (Stroud: Amberley
Publishing, 2022).

Downing, Lisa. *Selfish Women* (Abingdon, Oxon; New York,
NY: Routledge, 2019).

Feeney, Paul. *Baby Boomer Generation: A Lifetime of Memories*
(Stroud: The History Press Ltd, 2015).

Friedan, Betty. *The Feminine Mystique* (Harmondsworth:
Penguin, 1965).

Furlong, Andy, John Goodwin, Sarah Hadfield, et al. *Young People in the Labour Market: Past, Present, Future* (New York: Routledge, 2017).

Gillard, Derek. *Education in England: A History* (© Derek Gillard, 2018): www.educationengland.org.uk/history

Greenland, Katy. 'The repeal of Section 28', *Pastoral Care in Education* 26 (4) (November 2008): 243–251.

Greer, Germaine. *The Female Eunuch* (London: Flamingo, 1999 [1970]).

Hadow, Sir Henry. 'The Education of the Adolescent' (London: HM Stationery Office, 1926).

Harrington, Mary. *Feminism Against Progress* (Corbridge: Forum Books, 2023).

Ingham, Mary. *Now We Are Thirty* (London: Methuen, 1981).

———. *Facing Forty* (unpublished manuscript).

Institute for Fiscal Studies. 'Higher Education Funding in England: Past, Present and Options for the Future' (2017): https://ifs.org.uk/uploads/publications/bns/BN211.pdf

Jennings, Paul. *A History of Drink and the English, 1500–2000* (London: Routledge, 2016).

Lukianoff, Greg and Jonathan Haidt. *The Coddling of the American Mind* (New York: Penguin, 2018).

McCormick, John. *Contemporary Britain* (Basingstoke: Palgrave Macmillan, 2012).

Milne, A.A. *Now We Are Six* (London: Methuen, 1926).

Novarra, Virginia. *Women's Work, Men's Work: The Ambivalence of Equality* (London: Boyars, 1980).

Penny, Laurie. *Sexual Revolution: Modern Fascism and the Feminist Fightback* (London: Bloomsbury, 2022).

Perry, Louise. *The Case Against the Sexual Revolution* (Cambridge: Polity, 2022).

Scott, Jacqueline, Shirley Dex, and Heather Joshi. *Women and Employment* (Cheltenham: Edward Elgar Publishing, 2008).

Pinker, Steven. *How the Mind Works* (New York: Norton, 2009).

Rees, Gareth E. *Unofficial Britain: Journeys Through Unexpected Places* (London: Elliott & Thompson, 2020).

Rivett, Geoffrey. *The History of the NHS* (London: Nuffield Trust, 2019).

Sauerteig, Lutz and Roger Davidson. *Shaping Sexual Knowledge: A Cultural History of Sex Education in Twentieth Century Europe* (London: Routledge, 2007).

Selin Davis, Lisa. *Tomboy: The Surprising History and Future of Girls Who Dare to Be Different* (New York: Grand Central Publishing, 2021).

Siegler, A.M. and A. Grunebaum. 'The 100th anniversary of tubal sterilization', *Fertility and Sterility* 34 (6) (December 1980): 610–613.

Skenazy, Lenore. *Free-Range Kids: How to Raise Safe, Self-Reliant Children* (San Francisco: Jossey-Bass, 2010).

Sondheimer, Janet and P.R. Bodington. *The Girls' Public Day School Trust, 1872–1972: A Centenary Review* (London: Girls' Public Day School Trust, 1972).

Stack, Megan K. *Women's Work: A Personal Reckoning with Labour, Motherhood, and Privilege* (London: Le Scribe, 2019).

Thane, Pat and Tanya Evans. *Sinners? Scroungers? Saints? Unmarried Motherhood in Twentieth-Century England* (Oxford: Oxford University Press, 2012).

Todd, Selina. *The People: The Rise and Fall of the Working Class, 1910–2010* (London: John Murray, 2014).

———. *Snakes and Ladders: The Great British Social Mobility Myth* (London: Chatto & Windus, 2021).

Trollope, Joanna. *The Rector's Wife* (Cambridge: Black Swan, 1992).

Tunstall, Rebecca. *The Fall and Rise of Social Housing: 100 Years on 20 Estates* (Bristol: Policy Press, 2020).

Wassenaar, Ingrid. *Motherload: Modern Motherhood and How to Survive It* (London: IPW Books, 2022).

Wilson, Clive. *Time of My Life: A Jazz Journey from London to New Orleans* (Jackson: University Press of Mississippi, 2019).

Acknowledgements

I owe a special debt of thanks to the women whose personal thoughts and experiences I have mined to write this book. I am grateful for their permission to publish these stories, and very proud of what we have collectively achieved. The process of researching this book was made particularly enjoyable by the warm hospitality and genial welcome I received. There is something joyous about remembering your shared adolescence – a time long gone – with an old friend, over cups of tea or bottles of wine and plenty of raucous laughter.

Several people have helped with the practical side of things, from transcribing interviews to contributing ideas, reading bits of the manuscript, editing, typesetting, and cover design. Thank you to Brontë Schiltz, Laura Kincaid, Miranda Gill, Lisa Downing, Katharina Rietzler, Rachel Hamblin, Mary Ingham, Naomi Wilson, Mavis Wilson, Elizabeth Williams, and the whole Wilson family. Thanks also to my dearest friends and devoted writing buddies, Caroline Warman and Maya Mayblin.

I am grateful to the University of Warwick Humanities Research Ethics Committee, who offered advice at the planning stages, and to colleagues at Warwick (past and present) who have encouraged me in this sideline project. Any remaining errors, prejudices and insensitivities are my own.

Finally, my deepest gratitude is reserved for *my* family, for their unwavering love and support – to David, Nathaniel, and Genevieve.

In memory of my father, Mark Wilson (1946–2013).

About the Author

Susannah Wilson is a Reader (Associate Professor) in French Studies at the University of Warwick. Women's lives fascinate her and she is drawn to write about them. Her other books include *Voices from the Asylum: Four French Women Writers* (Oxford University Press, 2010). She has two children and lives in Oxford with her family and other animals.

Printed in Great Britain
by Amazon

25098510R00138